WOODEN GARDEN STRUCTURES

A COMPLETE GUIDE

WOODEN GARDEN STRUCTURES
A COMPLETE GUIDE

Mark Ekin

THE CROWOOD PRESS

First published in 2006 by
The Crowood Press Ltd
Ramsbury, Marlborough
Wiltshire SN8 2HR

www.crowood.com

British Library Cataloguing-in-Publication Data
A catalogue record for this book is available from the British Library.

ISBN 1 86126 837 8
EAN 978 1 86126 837 2

Acknowledgements
I am grateful to Sparsholt College, Winchester, where many of the photographs
were taken and would also like to thank Mark Winwood for his assistance and
help with some of the photographs. Finally, I would like to thank my wife Julie
for her love and support whilst writing and would especially like to acknowledge
the companionship given by Pip the Alsatian and Brecon the sheepdog who sat
with me well into the early hours on many occasions!

Line drawings by Keith Field.

Disclaimer
All tools and equipment used in building wooden garden structures of any kind
should be used in strict accordance with both the current health and safety
regulations and the manufacturer's instructions. The author and the publisher
do not accept any responsibility in any manner whatsoever for any error or
omission, or any loss, damage, injury, adverse outcome, or liability of any kind
incurred as a result of the use of any of the information contained in this book,
or reliance upon it. If in doubt about any aspect of the subjects covered in this
book, readers are advised to seek professional advice before embarking on any
installation or project.

Designed and typeset by Focus Publishing, 11a St Botolph's Road, Sevenoaks,
Kent TN13 3AJ

Printed and bound by The Cromwell Press, Trowbridge

Contents

CHAPTER 1

Introduction

Wood is one of our greatest natural renewable resources – it is environmentally friendly, has a natural beauty and offers a range of functional qualities. It is also an affordable resource that cannot be beaten by fabricated alternatives. The varieties of wood and their costs depend on where you live. There are approximately ten types of wood suitable for outside structures available from sustainable sources in the UK. This book looks at these and how they vary in natural appearance, robustness, durability and flexibility. It also demonstrates how they can be used in the construction process.

The choice of wood ultimately depends on what type of structure is to be built. Each chapter contains descriptions of specific designs that are intended to act as a template and to outline the basic principles and techniques. Once the various requirements and design have been finalized, the type of timber and fixings can be decided.

Softwoods, such as pine, are generally used to a far greater extent than hardwoods such as oak. This is mainly because softwoods are more readily available, cheaper and easier to use. Although both types of wood have their uses in outside construction, ultimately the choice is down to the person designing the structure. This book contains recommendations concerning the choice of materials, how various types of wood can be protected and how their appearance can be enhanced.

The aim of this book is to present a systematic guide to the construction of various wooden garden structures. It provides information and guidance to

OPPOSITE: The English woodland, which is the home of our timber resources.

RIGHT: A timber yard where the wood is cut into planks and other usable pieces of timber.

anyone who is interested their design, construction and maintenance, and will be of value to the keen DIY enthusiast, professional landscaper and garden designer. In each of the chapters there are projects to suit a variety of budgets, and in each case detailed instructions are provided, accompanied by explanatory photographs. For the more complex designs, step-by-step photographs or drawings are included that show the structures at each stage in the construction process.

METRIC AND IMPERIAL DIMENSIONS

The metric system has been used in the UK since the 1970s, although the imperial system of measurement is still in common practice. Therefore, both metric and imperial measurements appear in this book. However, if a designer or contractor is preparing a working document, the metric system should be used to avoid any possibility of confusion or inaccuracy.

BRITISH AND EUROPEAN TECHNICAL STANDARDS

In the construction of outdoor structures, all wood should be fully treated to enhance the long-term durability and appearance of the timber. Several British and European standards apply to such structures including:

- European Construction Products Directive 89/106/LEC (CPD). This states that building products, which includes wood for outdoor use, should exhibit adequate mechanical stability and strength throughout their design life. This basically means that designers and contractors have a clear legal duty to ensure that all the materials used in the construction have been tested.
- BS EN 350 (2 Parts): 1994. Presents information about the natural durability of named wooden species.
- BS EN 351 (2 Parts): 1994. Provides a vocabulary for contractors and designers to use when writing a specification concerning preservative protection requirements.
- BS EN 599 (2 Parts): 1997. Defines the formal

efficacy assessment procedures regarding preservative treatment.
- BS 5268: Part 5: 1989. Provides guidance on the preservation of structural timber for use in buildings in the UK. Relevant, but likely to be withdrawn.
- BS 5589: 1989. A guide to the specification and use of treated timber in the UK. Relevant, but also likely to be withdrawn.
- National Building Specification Z 12. Concerns preservative and fire-retardant treatments.
- National House Building Council (NHBC) Standards Chapter 2.3. Deals with natural solid timber preservation.

PLANNING CONTROLS

There are many different types of buildings and structures within the garden. As a general rule, a planning application is required if:

- The building or structure to be erected is nearer to any highway than the nearest part of the original house, unless there are at least 20m (65ft) between the building and the highway. Therefore, it is essential before you start planning to build any structure that you check to see if a road or footpath runs near the property, and if so, how far away it is from the structure, as this will determine whether planning permission is needed.
- More than half of the land around the house would be covered by the structure.
- The structure is to be used for running a business or storing commercial goods.
- The height of the structure is more than 3m (10ft), or 4m (13ft) if it has a rigid roof.
- The house is a listed building.
- The structure is in a conservation area and more than 10 cubic metres in volume.
- There is a condition attached to any planning permission for the property that restricts the building of any structures.

The above information only represents a guide and if there is any doubt whatsoever about the legality of a proposed structure, the local planning office should be contacted.

BOUNDARY LAW

When considering erecting new fencing or replacing old fencing, it is imperative that the ownership and precise location of the boundary is determined first. The starting point should be the title deeds to the house, which will contain a scale plan showing the boundaries of the gardens. A copy of any title deeds, not just your own, can be obtained confidentially from HM Land Registry.

The boundary plan gives a general indication of the boundaries and any 'T' marks on the plan point in the direction of the owner who has to maintain the boundary. However, in some cases, the plans may not state whose responsibility the boundary is. Notwithstanding this, ownership can usually be established – if the posts are on one side, ownership belongs to that garden. In the case of decorative fencing, ownership belongs to the side that the most ornate side of the fence is facing. Nonetheless, where there is any doubt it is best to consult with the neighbours and, if an agreement cannot be reached concerning the precise location and ownership of the boundary, legal assistance should be sought to prevent any disputes.

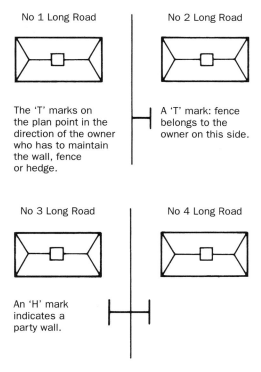

A boundary plan showing ownership and responsibility.

BRIEF HISTORICAL BACKGROUND

Woodworking can be defined as the process of turning wood/timber into an end product such as a structure or building, a piece of furniture or a carving.

Wood was one of the first materials worked by primitive man, and the development of civilization is closely allied to the advancement of skills related to working wood and other readily available natural resources such as stone, mud, and animal parts. Some of the earliest archaeological finds are the worked sticks from Kalambo Falls, Clacton-on-Sea and Lehringen.

Carved wooden vessels dating from Neolithic times have been found all over the world. There are also examples of Bronze Age woodcarvings including trees worked into wooden coffins and wooden folding chairs. There is also extensive evidence that wood was a major building material in the Iron Age – within prehistoric farms and settlements, the majority of the buildings were constructed from wood and the surrounding area was enclosed by a wooden fence. A good example of this can be seen at Butser ancient farm near Portsmouth. There have also been numerous finds of the flint tools used for carving wood.

Woodworking also took place in the ancient civilizations of Egypt and China. The originators of Chinese woodworking are believed to have been Lu Ban and his wife Lady Yun. Lu Ban is credited with the invention of the chalk-line, plane, and other woodworking tools. The book *Lu Ban Jing* is supposed to be a record of his teachings but this seems doubtful as it was written approximately one and a half centuries after his death! Notwithstanding this, the book is filled with specifications for the construction of a variety of structures from flower-pots to tables and temples.

In all parts of the world, timber has been a widely

ABOVE: *The rooftops of Butser ancient farm near Portsmouth.*

LEFT: *The site of a cruck truss cottage or house at Wirksworth, Derbyshire, probably dating from the late medieval period.*

BELOW: *An archway at Carsington Water, Derbyshire that represents the frame of a Bronze Age house.*

used building material and timber-framed buildings can be traced back through the centuries. In England, for example, the cruck frame, one of the earliest types of frame used in buildings, was in use over six hundred years ago. This was made up of an oak trunk sawn in half, which was then constructed into an 'A'-frame, linked with horizontal timbers. The 'A'-frame was then in-filled with hazel or willow fencing and covered with wattle and daub, which is a mixture of mud, straw, and cow dung. Many of the 'A'-frame structures that still exist have now been in-filled with brick or stone.

One of the oldest wooden structures in the world is the Horyu-ji temple in Japan, which was built around the start of the eighth century. In Europe, there are some good surviving examples of early wooden structures – some of the best ones being the unique twelfth- and fourteenth-century Stave Churches in Norway, one of the most famous of which is Urnesstavkirke which is on the UNESCO world heritage list.

Even today, some buildings, such as Saint Thomas More Church at Weake near Winchester, are still being built entirely from timber. There are specialist companies that not only make the smaller structures such as sheds and summerhouses, but also larger buildings, some of which have two storeys and can be used for a variety of purposes.

The first use of wooden structures within gardens can be traced back to the Egyptian domestic gardens, which were surprisingly like our own and used for similar activities such as relaxation, outdoor eating, play and the cultivation of both ornamental and edible plants. The structure of these gardens can be seen in the Egyptian tomb paintings. The ancient Egyptian gardens were traditionally rectangular enclosures with high walls. The garden itself was intended as an outside living area and consisted of fruit trees, flowers, pools and pot plants. One of the first types of wooden garden structure was the pergola, which was usually covered in vines, and designed so that the garden could be enjoyed all the year round.

The Romans also valued gardens and brought

Thomas More Church at Weake, Winchester, Hampshire.

them into the centre of the house, making them an important part of domestic life. These were formal gardens, made up of flowerbeds, paths, water gardens and statuary. The Romans also built pergolas and there is some evidence that they attempted to build an early form of conservatory that would let in the light but keep out the cold using mica instead of glass.

After the fall of the Roman Empire, few developments took place in European gardens for many centuries. However, monastic gardens continued to be developed, the main function of which was food production. As for the introduction of new structures within the garden, there is a plan that derives from the ninth century of the monastery of St Gall in Switzerland that shows a total of thirty-three raised beds.

The crooked spire of St Mary's and All Saints Church dominates the skyline at Chesterfield, Derbyshire.

In the sixteenth century, Europe became more peaceful and formal garden plans were devised leading to the development of structures such as wooden trellises and archways. Also during this century, oranges were introduced into Britain – the first pips being brought in along with the potato. With the introduction of oranges, a new wooden structure was invented in the form of the early greenhouse. These structures were constructed from timber with some glazing, which included wooden panels that could be removed to let in light and warmth on milder days but could be replaced on colder days and nights. Subsequently, these structures were further developed not only as greenhouses, but also as conservatories.

Prior to the mid-nineteenth century, timber preservatives were seldom used in garden wooden structures apart from the occasional use of substances such as lime, linseed oil or wood tar. Green timber, however, was frequently used. Freshly cut and unseasoned, it is easy to work with because it is much softer than seasoned wood. As it dries, green timber becomes much stronger and turns very hard. Its big disadvantage is that it is impossible to know how it will dry, and defects can appear and develop, especially when used inside wooden structures. A good example of this may be seen at St Mary and All Saints Church at Chesterfield, Derbyshire. It is believed that the spire became crooked because green timber was used in its construction.

Most timber used in construction nowadays, especially outdoors, is seasoned and preserved. One of the first preservatives was the specially patented mercury chloride (calomel), which was first introduced in 1860 as a treatment for preventing rot and worm infestation. Creosote was also used in the nineteenth century along with salts of copper, chrome and boron. It is probably true to say that the majority of wood used since the mid-nineteenth century has been treated with one, or more of these chemicals. The choice of chemical used in preservative treatments is usually based on its stability and durability, which means that such chemicals can remain in the timber almost indefinitely. The majority of these are slightly volatile and can slowly release toxins into the atmosphere. This is the case with creosote, which has been banned for

The thatched entrance to the wood fair at the New Forest Show, Hampshire.

public use since 2003, as research has concluded that the active ingredient, benzo-a-pyrene, may have a greater potential to cause cancer than was previously thought.

Timber and timber construction is as important today as ever and it continues play an important role in construction. The use of wood and wooden structures within the garden is common practice. For many households, the modern garden forms an important part of the living area. Recently, there has been a renaissance of interest in gardens and outdoor living, due mainly due to increased media coverage coupled with the fact that the pursuit of a healthy lifestyle now forms an important part of modern living. Also, people now live much longer, retire earlier, and generally have more leisure time to spend in their gardens, not just gardening but also relaxing and pursuing various leisure activities. The modern garden must, therefore, meet a variety of needs and wooden structures can help fulfil some of these – fences for privacy, summerhouses for relaxation, and sheds for storage to name but a few.

TRADITIONAL WOODCRAFTS IN THE UK

The word coppice derives from the French word *couper* (to cut). Coppiced trees and their produce are known as underwood. Coppicing can be defined as the process of cutting trees down to stumps and allowing these to generate new growth, which is then left for between eight and thirty years, depending on the species and end use. After this period the resulting stems are harvested. The tree species used include hazel, willow, oak, sweet chestnut, maple, ash and lime

Coppicing is the oldest form of woodland management. There is archaeological evidence of coppicing at Fishbourne on the Isle of Wight, where a hazel wattle trackway was discovered that dates back to 3500BC. Coppiced poles, approximately six thousand years old, have been excavated in Somerset where they were used to build wetland trackways. In addition to this, woven hazel screens, which were used for fishing, have been found dating back to 5000BC.

A traditional craftsman at work.

A willow hurdle being made.

Coppiced woods are usually cut on a rotating cycle, typically seven to eight years for trees such as hazel, because many traditional uses require eight-year-old material. However, it has been known for some rotational cycles to be up to thirty years for species such as oak where larger material is required. One commonly used form of management was known as 'coppice with standards', which was a two-tier system with lower-growing, closely spaced hazel trees and an upper layer of widely spaced oak 'standards', which were allowed to grow as single-stemmed trees.

Coppicing and the traditional crafts associated with it were still widely practised until the Second World War. After this time, many coppices fell into disrepair as modern, less labour-intensive forestry systems were adopted. However, in recent times there has been a resurgence in coppicing and traditional woodcrafts. There are now estimated to be four hundred working craftsmen in the UK, particularly in the south of England; and countryside and wood fairs are becoming commonplace. Some of the traditional products such as hazel hurdles are now included in many landscape designs and can be used either on their own or as part of a structure.

CHAPTER 2

Wood, Preservatives, Colourants, Fixings and Tools

TYPES OF WOOD AND THEIR USES

Wood can be classified into two categories: hardwoods and softwoods. However, this classification can be misleading because many hardwoods, such as balsa, can be of a fairly soft texture. Conversely, several of the softwoods are quite hard. The reason for these apparent contradictions lies in the botanical classification of trees that divides them into two main groups: angiosperms and gymnosperms. The angiosperms are trees with broad leaves such as oak, mahogany, ash and teak – these are referred to as hardwoods. The gymnosperms are trees whose leaves usually have needles such as pines, firs and spruces – these are referred to as softwoods.

Oak (Quercus robur).

Scots pine (Pinus sylvestris).

The main differences between hardwoods and softwoods are to be found in their appearance – hardwoods being generally more colourful. The other feature is durability – hardwoods have a natural durability and do not need to be pressure treated (tanalized). Introduced approximately thirty years ago, tanalizing makes softwoods impervious to damp and fungal decay, which can make them last for between forty and fifty years in damp ground conditions – as long as some hardwoods. Moreover, with the introduction of a vast range of colorants, they can also look as good as many of the hardwoods.

As a general rule, the majority of the softwoods are easier to work with. They are also reasonably priced and widely available. One of the main reasons why softwoods are easier to obtain is that hardwood trees are much slower growing. It should be stressed that it is always important to ensure that all your wood, especially hardwood timber, comes from a renewable resource.

There are many different types of timber but only a few of these are used commercially. The following list indicates types of wood available in the UK and many parts of Europe for outdoor timber structures. It also outlines their general appearance and characteristics. The average density of each of the different types of wood is shown, expressed in its weight per kilogram.

Hardwoods

American Mahogany (*Swietenia spp*)

Also known as British Honduras mahogany, Central American mahogany, bay wood, Cuban, or Spanish mahogany. It has a good natural colour, ranging from a yellowish brown to a deep, rich red. The timber is easy to work with, takes screws and nails well and gives an excellent finish. The density of mahogany varies – the average density of Honduras mahogany is about $540kg/m^3$, whereas the average density of Cuban mahogany is $770kg/m^3$. Mahogany is easily obtainable in many sizes, has a good decorative appearance and is highly resistant to decay, which makes it very suitable for high-class joinery and boat building. It is also a good choice when considering a hardwood timber for garden structures.

Oak (*Quercus robur* and *Quercus petraea*)

This is probably the most useful of hardwood timbers and is often selected for constructing wooden structures where a hardwood is specified. It is a pale, yellowish brown with a distinctive darker outline. English oak is the hardest and toughest oak timber, whilst Polish or Slovenian oak is usually the softest and easiest to work with. The workability of oak varies according to whether the timber is fast or slow grown. A well-seasoned oak withstands decay well

Timber – be it softwood or hardwood – can be used to create a simple structure or something more unusual, as this children's play area demonstrates.

and has good resistance to fire. It is classed as a heavy wood and has a density of approximately 690kg/m³ depending on the type of oak. Oak has many uses as a material for garden structures and can be used both for heavy construction work and for building such structures as high-quality fences and gates. One of the main problems with oak is that it tends to contain a large amount of acid, which corrodes iron, therefore steel screws and fixings should be avoided. Also, because of the high acid contact, it reacts badly against casein glues and other alkaline materials. However, using the correct glues, it does glue easily and has an excellent decorative appearance.

Teak *(Tectona grandis)*

When freshly cut, this timber is greenish yellow in colour but as it ages it becomes golden brown in appearance with an attractive dark outline. The pungent leathery smell of this wood is very distinctive. Teak is extremely durable and is resistant to insects, acids and fire. The texture is greasy and gritty and because of this, tools tend to become blunted quickly. Teak is hard and strong and is quite an even timber to work with despite its blunting aspect. It glues well, especially with polyvinyl acetate and urea resin adhesives but nails and screw pilot holes are also required. When working with this timber, dust masks should be used and it should be worked in a well-ventilated area, because the fine dust produced is a known irritant. Teak has a density of 640kg/m³, and therefore is ideal for use when building wooden structures.

Softwoods

Douglas Fir *(Pseudotsuga taxifolia)*

Also known as British Columbian pine and Oregon pine. This is a strong and flexible wood that has a good natural resistance to decay. It is pinkish brown in colour, has a clean sweet smell and a very distinct grain. Douglas fir is a fairly easy timber to work with – it saws easily, can be nailed or screwed and also glues quite well. However, it can sometimes split when being nailed or tacked. Therefore, where strength or visual appearance is essential it may be best to avoid the use of nails or pins. Also, because of its grain and the tendency for resin to bleed from the

A newly cut softwood board.

wood, it is not the best timber to paint; therefore it is best to apply either the wood stain or varnish. Douglas Fir is a medium density timber at 540kg/m³ and can be used for heavy as well as general construction work in the garden.

Larch *(Larix deciduous)*

A fairly new commercially available timber, which is reddish-brown in colour with a pale sapwood and a generally straight grain. The timber is strong and very durable. It is not suitable for joinery or interior use, and is mainly used for gates, fences, garden and farm buildings and rustic work. It is classed as a medium density timber at 580kg/m³. Although it easy to work – it saws well, and takes nails, screws and glues fairly easily – it is resinous and does not take a painted finish too well because the resin bleeds through, therefore a wood stained or varnished finish is recommended.

Redwood *(Pinus sylvestrus)*

Also known as yellow pine, Scots pine, common pine or red deal. This is a pinkish white timber with an orange-red grain, clearly marked rings and a distinct, clean pine smell. It is a resinous timber and knots are nearly always present. It is an easy timber to work with, being easy to nail, screw and glue. The timber is

Poorly stacked boards can cause bowing.

quite strong and straight grained with a moderately good natural resistance to decay. It is a medium density timber at 500kg/m³. This timber can be brought to a fine finish, and takes both varnish and paint very well. Redwood is probably one of the most popular softwoods in the UK and can be incorporated within most structures in the garden.

Western Red Cedar *(Thuja plicata)*

This is a straight-grained, soft and spongy timber with few knots. It is a pink, reddish brown but turns grey when exposed to the weather. It is one of the lighter timbers with a density of 380kg/m³. It is non-resinous and requires sharp tools to give a good finish. It has a natural resistance to decay and is ideal for use on outside structures. In fact, one of its main uses is for external cladding of sheds and other wooden buildings. However, it is not strong enough for use in heavy structural work. The timber takes paint, varnish and wood stain well, and is easily nailed, screwed or glued. Where possible, iron fixings should be avoided as they may cause staining and corrosion.

CHOOSING A WOOD

When selecting softwood in particular, try to choose the timber that has the lightest growth rings as this means that it is from the middle of the trunk where the best wood can be found. Always try to choose the straightest and flattest wood, avoiding anything with many knot holes as they are very difficult to cut and drill. The other defects a purchaser should be aware of are:

Blue Stain

Blue stain is a blue-grey discolouration of the timber that occurs mainly in the lighter-coloured softwoods. It is caused by a fungus that lives on the food stored within living cells and it is therefore confined to the sapwood. The defect itself is not serious, but it does indicate that there is a large amount of sapwood in the affected timber, which is not desirable when using timber for construction purposes.

Bowing

Bowing is usually caused by poor stacking of boards although it can also be caused by internal stresses within the tree being released after it has been converted into workable timber.

Case Hardening

Case hardening occurs mainly with kiln-dried timbers that are 5cm (2in) or more in thickness and is characterized by the two surfaces of the board becoming concave. This is caused by the timber drying too quickly in the early stages of seasoning, which results in the outside cells becoming dried and hardened, allowing moisture to remain in the centre of the timber and build up stresses within the wood. When the timber is subsequently re-cut, these stresses are released and this causes the concave distortions.

Collapse

Collapse only occurs in kiln-dried timber and is the result of over-rapid drying, often at temperatures that are too high. This causes moisture to be lost from the centre of the board more quickly than air can replace it. This, in turn, causes the cells to collapse giving the board an uneven wave-like appearance.

End splits

End splits are caused by the wood drying too quickly.

Knots

Knots occur mainly in softwood and they mark the origin of a branch. Knots can be classed either as live or dead. This terminology signifies the condition of the branch that caused it. Small, sound, live knots have no detrimental effect on the timber and in some situations can enhance its appearance. However, dead knots, which are invariably loose and larger knots, live or dead, can cause structural weakness. As a general rule when installing timber joists, the joist should be placed where possible with the knots at the topside of the joist because knots on the lower side can have a weakening effect (*see* diagram below). It should also be noted that the weakening effect of a knot is reduced when it is near the end of a joist.

Short Grain

This term applies to timber where the grain curves and is not parallel to the longitudinal axis of the wood. This defect is usually caused by a natural growth disorder. In the majority of wood there will be some degree of short grain because not many tree trunks are absolutely straight. The problem with short-grained timber is that it breaks easily and therefore it should be avoided if it is to be used in any loadbearing capacity.

Springing

Springing is where there is a curvature on the edges of the board. It is usually due to internal stresses that are released during seasoning. This is not usually serious and in fact when constructing some structures, small amounts of springing can be used to advantage because it counteracts a natural tendency of the wood to sag.

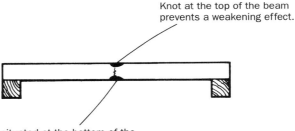

Knot at the top of the beam prevents a weakening effect.

If the knot is situated at the bottom of the beam, the weight can cause the beam to crack.

The possible weakening effect of a knot on the lower side of a joist.

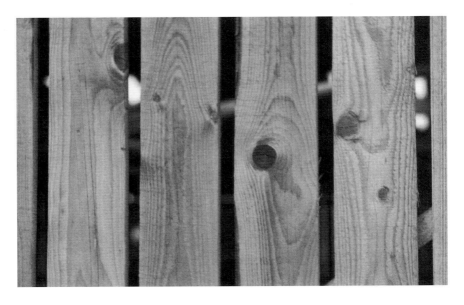

Knots in wood are not always a problem, they can also be decorative and add to its beauty.

Surface Checking

Surface checking is where small longitudinal splits occur on both the face and ends of the board. These are caused either by warmth from the sun, or frost, on air-dried timber. These are not serious structural defects but they do spoil the appearance of the wood.

Twists

Twists are caused by poor seasoning, bad stacking or by the release of internal stresses when the timber is converted to usable wood.

Upsets

Upsets occur mostly in tropical woods, with mahogany being the most susceptible. It is usually caused by bad felling, for example when the tree is felled across a hard raised surface such as a fallen log. A hairline crack develops within the wood, which is very serious as the wood can be broken easily. This problem is very difficult to detect until the timber is planed.

Waney Edge

Waney edge occurs where the edges of the timber start to decrease in size and can cause weakness, especially in timber used for construction.

Warping or Cupping

Warping or cupping is very common in boards and is caused by shrinkage of the wood when it is drying or as a result of a dry board absorbing moisture. Another problem which occurs is in boards that are 5cm (2in) or thicker, because as the wood warps it tends to crack on the convex side.

SAWN AND PLANED TIMBER

Sawn timber is rough in appearance and is measured as it is cut from the tree, which means that the measurements are not exact and shrinkage should be allowed for. Planed timber is smooth and approximately 5mm (³⁄₁₆in) smaller all round than the sawn size. Traditionally, planed timber was sold by its sawn size, however, it is now common practice for suppliers to put the true size of the timber in brackets after the sawn size, with the word 'nominal' following the measurement.

STANDARD TIMBER SIZES

Unlike hardwoods, softwoods are readily available from DIY shops. The table opposite shows what sizes of softwood timber are commonly available. The sizes refer to the sawn timber sizes.

Softwood timber is sold in standard metric lengths of 1.8m (6ft), increasing by 30cm (12in) up to 6.3m (20 ft 8in).

SECOND-HAND TIMBER

The main advantage of second-hand timber is that it is relatively cheap and readily available from demolition, salvage and reclaimed material merchants. However, because it is second-hand, it should be

A pile of second-hand timber ready for re-use.

Standard Sawn Timber Sizes Most Commonly Used and Readily Available in the UK

Thickness	Width	Planed	Sawn	Thickness	Width	Planed	Sawn
12mm (½in)	2.5cm (1in)	Yes	Yes	3.2cm (1¼in)	3.2cm (1¼in)	Yes	No
12mm (½in)	3.8cm (1½in)	Yes	No	3.2cm (1¼in)	3.8cm (1½in)	Yes	No
12mm (½in)	5cm (2in)	Yes	Yes	3.2cm (1¼in)	5cm (2in)	Yes	Yes
12mm (½in)	7.5cm (3in)	Yes	Yes	3.2cm (1¼in)	7.5cm (3in)	Yes	Yes
12mm (½in)	10cm (4in)	Yes	Yes	3.2cm (1¼in)	10cm (4in)	Yes	Yes
12mm (½in)	15cm (6in)	Yes	No	3.2cm (1¼in)	11.5cm (4½in)	Yes	No
				3.2cm (1¼in)	13cm (5in)	Yes	Yes
16mm (⅝in)	2.5cm (1in)	Yes	No	3.2cm (1¼in)	14cm (5½in)	Yes	No
16mm (⅝in)	3.8cm (1½in)	Yes	No	3.2cm (1¼in)	15cm (6in)	Yes	Yes
16mm (⅝in)	5cm (2in)	Yes	No	3.2cm (1¼in)	17.5cm (7in)	Yes	Yes
16mm (⅝in)	7.5cm (3in)	Yes	No	3.2cm (1¼in)	20cm (8in)	No	Yes
16mm (⅝in)	10cm (4in)	Yes	No	3.2cm (1¼in)	23cm (9in)	No	Yes
19mm (¾in)	2.5cm (1in)	Yes	Yes	3.8cm (1½in)	3.8cm (1½in)	Yes	Yes
19mm (¾in)	3.8cm (1½in)	Yes	Yes	3.8cm (1½in)	5cm (2in)	Yes	Yes
19mm (¾in)	5cm (2in)	Yes	Yes	3.8cm (1½in)	7.5cm (3in)	Yes	Yes
19mm (¾in)	7.5cm (3in)	Yes	Yes	3.8cm (1½in)	10cm (4in)	Yes	Yes
19mm (¾in)	10cm (4in)	No	Yes	3.8cm (1½in)	13cm (5in)	No	Yes
19mm (¾in)	13cm (5in)	Yes	Yes	3.8cm (1½in)	15cm (6in)	Yes	Yes
19mm (¾in)	15cm (6in)	Yes	Yes	3.8cm (1½in)	17.5cm (7in)	No	Yes
19mm (¾in)	17.5cm (7in)	Yes	Yes	3.8cm (1½in)	20cm (8in)	No	Yes
19mm (¾in)	23cm (9in)	Yes	Yes	3.8cm (1½in)	23cm (9in)	Yes	Yes
22mm (⅞in)	3.2cm (1¼in)	Yes	No	5cm (2in)	5cm (2in)	Yes	Yes
22mm (⅞in)	5cm (2in)	Yes	No	5cm (2in)	7.5cm (3in)	Yes	Yes
22mm (⅞in)	7.5cm (3in)	Yes	No	5cm (2in)	10cm (4in)	Yes	Yes
22mm (⅞in)	10cm (4in)	Yes	No	5cm (2in)	13cm (5in)	Yes	Yes
				5cm (2in)	15cm (6in)	Yes	Yes
2.5cm (1in)	2.5cm (1in)	Yes	Yes	5cm (2in)	17.5cm (7in)	Yes	Yes
2.5cm (1in)	3.8cm (1½in)	Yes	Yes	5cm (2in)	20cm (8in)	Yes	Yes
2.5cm (1in)	5cm (2in)	Yes	Yes	5cm (2in)	23cm (9in)	Yes	Yes
2.5cm (1in)	7.5cm (3in)	Yes	Yes				
2.5cm (1in)	10cm (4in)	Yes	Yes	7.5cm (3in)	7.5cm (3in)	Yes	Yes
2.5cm (1in)	13cm (5in)	Yes	Yes	7.5cm (3in)	10cm (4in)	Yes	Yes
2.5cm (1in)	15cm (6in)	Yes	Yes	7.5cm (3in)	13cm (5in)	No	Yes
2.5cm (1in)	17.5cm (7in)	Yes	Yes	7.5cm (3in)	15cm (6in)	No	Yes
2.5cm (1in)	20cm (8in)	Yes	Yes	7.5cm (3in)	17.5cm (7in)	No	Yes
2.5cm (1in)	23cm (9in)	Yes	Yes	7.5cm (3in)	20cm (8in)	No	Yes
				7.5cm (3in)	23cm (9in)	No	Yes

inspected carefully to ensure that it does not have woodworm or rot. Also, it is likely to contain nails or screws and some wood such as old floorboards may contain grit that can blunt tools. Another disadvantage with second-hand timber is that a specific size cannot be guaranteed and you will have to cut it to size yourself. Also, with some woods, especially hardwood, a piece of wood may appear straight and flat but cutting it thinner may release tensions that can cause it to twist.

WOOD PRESERVATIVES AND COLORANTS

Timber is prone to both fungal and insect attack. However, in order for fungus and/or insects to live and multiply, they need four essentials – air, water, food and a suitable temperature. If they are deprived of these, the timber is safe from attack.

There are two main measures that can be taken to help protect timber from attack and decay. First, keep the timber dry, which deprives the organisms of water. While this is very useful against fungal attack, it is not very effective against insects. The second measure, which will protect against both fungal and insect attack, is to deprive the organisms of food, and this done by poisoning the wood. In this case, the use of chemical preservatives is the most effective method of control. However, the majority of timber sold for outdoor use is pre-treated. It is also worth noting that timber sold as untreated will probably have been sprayed with an anti-sap stain chemical, which is used to prevent blue-black staining moulds. This preventative treatment does not penetrate too deeply into the wood; therefore if a totally uncontaminated timber, free of preservative is required, heavy sanding will be the answer.

Preservatives can be applied or introduced to timber using any of the following methods:

- Pressure-treatment or tanalization, where preservative is forced into the timber under pressure, is the method used on the majority of pre-treated timber. It is estimated to prevent timber degradation for at least twenty years even when the timber is in the ground
- Dipping or immersing in an open tank for a short period then allowing the wood to dry. This method is used for items such as fence panels prior to sale. It can also be used on the bases of posts prior to putting them in the ground to give added protection.
- Brushing will help to maintain and preserve previously installed surfaces. It can also be used for applying wood stains and should be applied liberally.
- Spraying is used for a similar purpose to brushing and should be applied with a coarse spray.

Exterior-Quality Paints and Varnishes

Paints and varnishes protect timber from water penetration and abrasive particles. Paint has the added advantage of protecting wood from solar radiation. If paint or varnish is applied correctly and the finished surface is not damaged, it should give quite good protection for up to five years. Gloss paints can be used for outdoor structures but these have now been largely superseded by high-quality acrylic primers and sealants because these have the following benefits that are essential in any paint that is to be used outside:

- Adhesion – sticks to the wood surface without blistering, peeling or flaking.
- Breathing – when dry, this allows moisture within the wood to escape without causing blistering or damage to the paint surface.
- Chalk resistance – the film of the paint resists erosion of the surface, which would result in a powdery formation.
- Colour retention – the colour is retained for a long period of time without fading.
- Flexibility – the coating stretches with the natural expansion and contraction of the wood. Without this, the paint is likely to split or crack, which will then allow moisture to penetrate the wood.
- Mildew resistance – the paint has a resistance to fungal growth on its surface, which can be unsightly and difficult to remove.

Water-Repellent Exterior Stains

Stains can give either a clear or coloured, matt or semi-gloss, water-repellent surface and, because of their wood preservative content, they can give protection against decay for up to four years. Stains let the wood grain show through and allow it to breathe so any trapped moisture can escape; whereas paint can become trapped and damage the surface, allowing moisture to penetrate, which can then get trapped and rot the wood.

Creosote (Tar Oil)

Creosote has been a popular form of preservative for many years. However, since 30 June 2003, laws have come in that prohibit the public use of creosote, as research has shown that there is a cancer risk. However, it should be noted that timber treated prior to this date may be still used in the garden as long as there is no frequent skin contact.

A selection of wooden buildings, some coloured with light stain and others with darker stain.

Water-Borne Preservatives

These consist mainly of salts of copper, zinc, mercury or chromium, dissolved in water. They have good powers of penetration into timber, they are fairly inexpensive, very toxic to fungi and insects, and have no adverse effect on the application of paint or glues.

Organic Solvent Preservatives

The most effective of the preservatives, but also the most costly. Organic solvent preservatives are made up of various chemicals dissolved in a spirit base, which can be volatile. They have excellent penetrating qualities, do not have an adverse effect on the application of paint or glue, and dry out quickly so that the timber does not swell and become distorted. Methods of application include brushing, spraying, immersion, and certain pressure processes.

Polythene Sleeve and Bituminous Sealants

This system is ideal where untreated or dip-treated posts are used – for example in rustic work. With this system, the base of the post is inserted into a polythene sleeve using a machine. The machine then heats the sleeve and melts the bituminous sealant so it is in contact with the post and also shrinks the polythene to provide a tight fit around it. The post can then be set in the ground and forms a strong barrier, which prevents decay. However, it is essential that 5cm (2in) of the post is left above the ground to prevent the entry of any surface water.

FIXINGS AND THEIR USES

Nails

Nails are one of the oldest fixings, having been around for thousands of years. The first types were heat forged, but when machinery was introduced, they were superseded by ones cut from sheets of metal. Most nails used today are cut from rolls of wire.

Nails are usually either steel, stainless steel or galvanized (zinc-plated) – the last two being used mainly in outdoor construction because of their resistance to rust. In the majority of cases, galvanized nails are the best choice because stainless steel can react with the tannins in certain woods, such as oak, and cause staining. Regular wooden nails are commonly referred to as wire nails, and although points can vary, the four-sided diamond point is the one most frequently used. The heads can differ, with the smaller heads often being chosen as they are not easily visible and can be painted over. However, larger, corrugated-headed nails help to prevent the hammer from slipping and also reduce the risk of damage to the wood.

Although nails are widely used, they do not hold wood together as strongly as screws. However, their holding power can be enhanced by:

- An adhesive coating that heats up as the nail is driven into the wood – as it cools, the bond solidifies and becomes stronger.
- A nail shaft with rings, spirals or barbs, so that they bind into the wood fibres for better holding power. However, it should be noted that once these types of nails have been used, they become very difficult to remove, and even if you are successful in removing them, the wood will be damaged.

It is important when selecting a type of nail for a particular job that the right size is chosen – as a general rule, the nail should be at least two and a half times longer than the thickness of the timber to be held, and the rule of nailing thinner timber to thicker timber should always be observed.

In the case of nailing wood to masonry, the masonry nail should be driven more than 19mm (¾in) into the surface of the wood. When the nail is to be driven through a plastered surface, the thickness of the plaster should be added to the thickness of the wood in order to calculate the size of nail required.

The following guidelines should be observed when using nails:

- To strengthen the fixing power of a nail, it should be driven in at an angle – especially important when fixing into end grain.

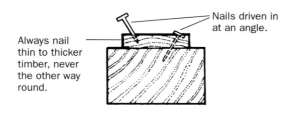

Always nail thin to thicker timber, never the other way round.

Nails driven in at an angle.

Nails should be driven in at an angle to strengthen the fixing power.

If nails are not blunted before driving in then splitting can occur.

- With harder wood such as oak, guide holes should be drilled that are just a fraction smaller than the nail to be used.

There are two methods that can be used to prevent bouncing when driving in nails to join two pieces of unsupported timber:

- Where possible, with the piece of wood, which is to be supported, it is best to hammer a nail, into it, first on a surface, so that the point is just short of the maximum width.
- Placing a heavy object behind the two pieces of wood to be joined together.

In order to avoid splits when hammering nails near the end of a piece of wood, it is best to cut it slightly longer than what is required and then the excess can be cut flush once the two pieces have been joined together. Also, it is best not to drive more than one nail into the same grain line. Another method that may be adopted when driving nails into timber that may split easily is to blunt the nail tip first by hitting it on a hard surface before driving it into the wood.

For some joinery work, where a decorative finish is

needed, there may be a requirement for the nails to be hidden. In this case, a thin sliver of wood should be lifted up using a chisel, and then the nail can be driven in. Afterwards it should be glued back and held in place with a 'G'-clamp.

Types of Nails and Their Uses

Clout
Length 19mm–10cm (¾–4in). Its large head makes it ideal for fencing and fixing roofing felt.

Lost Head
Length 2.5–15cm (1–6in). Available with a round or oval head that can be punched below the surface, making it a good choice where a neat finish is required.

Round Wire
Length 19mm–15cm (¾–6in). This general-purpose nail is used where strength is more important than a neat appearance. Its disadvantage is that it has a tendency to split some types of wood.

Oval Wire
Length 2.5–15cm (1–6in). Used for similar purposes as round wire nails, but less likely to split wood.

Masonry
Length 16mm–10cm (⅝–4in). Hardened steel for fixing wood directly to masonry, available in heavy and fine gauges.

Screw or Annular
Length 19mm–10cm (¾–4in). Good holding power – used for fastening sheet materials to wood.

Roofing
Length 2cm (⅜in). Used for fixing corrugated sheeting to roofing rafters.

Staple
Available in a numerous designs and sizes, predominately used for securing wire fencing.

Screws
Screws, like nails, are made from a variety of materials, the main ones being steel, stainless steel and brass. Like nails, they can be galvanized for rust resistance. Another type of finish that can be used to prevent rust is known as bluing, although it is actually black in colour. Again, it is best to avoid the use of steel because of its reaction to tannins in particular woods.

Screws are usually 15–20cm (6–8in) long. The

Staples can be used for securing wire fencing to wooden posts.

Screws come in a variety of sizes.

gauge of the screw shaft is rated by numbers 2–24, the higher gauge number indicating a larger screw.

Screws have a greater holding power than nails and can be removed from timber causing little or no damage. They come in two types.

Slotted
This has a single-groove screw head, and is used with a flat-head screwdriver.

Phillips or Cross-Headed
These have cross-slotted screw heads with either 'U'- or 'V'-shaped slots of uniform width, and are driven in with a Phillips screwdriver.

Screw Heads

Screws have three types of heads.

Flat
Used where the head needs to be flush with the surface.

Oval
The bottom half of this head is countersunk and the top is rounded, which gives a better appearance and makes it easier to remove than a flat-head screw.

Round
Used where the head needs to be level with the surface.

Threads

There are two types of thread associated with woodworking applications.

Fine
Best used for hardwoods

Coarse
Primarily used for softwoods.

Types of Screws and Their Uses

Wood
Designed for attaching wood to wood and can be made of stainless steel, galvanized or brass. Wood screws are available in the three head types – flat, oval or round, and can be either slotted-head or Phillips. These screws are threaded for three-quarters of the length, and it is always advisable to drill a pilot hole before using.

Deck
Used in outdoor situations where strength and resistance is important, such as in the construction of decking. The threads go all the way to the head and have their own self-drilling point, and are usually galvanized for outdoor applications.

Dowel
Used for the invisible fixing of end-to-end wood

Cross-headed screws used to secure hinges to a gate.

joints, it is threaded on both ends and the two pieces of wood are twisted together to tighten.

Coach
An extremely large wood screw of 10–15cm (4–6in) in length with a square head, which is tightened with a spanner. Used where maximum strength is required.

Screw Accessories

Flat Washers
Used for round head screws, they spread the load to give a tight grip.

Screw Cups (Raised Type)
Improve the appearance and help to spread the load.

Screw Cups (Socket Type)
Used for countersunk screws, screw cups are driven into a pre-drilled hole for a completely flush fitting.

Nuts

Types of Nuts and Their Uses

Hexagonal
The most commonly used nut, available in a wide range of sizes.

Square
This type of nut usually comes in large sizes only and therefore is traditionally used with the bigger types of bolts.

Wing
Used in situations where the nut must be undone quickly, it can be tightened and undone by hand.

Locking
Used in situations where vibration may make the nut come loose, it has a fibre ring inside, which prevents it from loosening.

Bolts

In the majority of cases, either screws or nails are the

A countersunk screw, screwed into a screw cup for a flush fitting.

preferred option for constructing exterior wooden structures. However, bolts can be used where:

- It is necessary to dismantle all or parts of the wooden structure occasionally.
- The structure needs to be secured to a solid surface, for example, concrete bolts, nuts, and washers for fitting wood to wood.

Types of Bolts and Their Uses

Coach
The coach bolt can be up to 50cm (20in), in length, with a diameter of 4–19mm (³⁄₁₆–³⁄₄in). It has a square collar under a domed head that locks into the wood as the bolt is turned, which means that only one spanner is required.

Machine
Available in the same sizes as the coach bolt but with a hexagonal or square flat head that does not lock into the wood, therefore two spanners are required.

Anchor bolts used to secure a post bracket to the concrete base.

Machine Screw
Notwithstanding its name, this is a bolt. Available only in smaller sizes of 6mm–5cm (¼–2in) in length and 1–6mm (³⁄₆₄–¼in) in diameter.

Washers for Use with Bolts

Washers are used on bolts, not just to ensure a tighter hold, but also to prevent the flat heads of the bolts and nuts from sinking into the wood. There are two types of washers used in timber construction:

Flat
Spreads the load to give a tighter grip and also makes the nuts easier to turn.

Toothed
Gripping teeth prevent the bolts from loosening. Ideal for use in situations where there is a risk of vibration.

Timber Connectors
In addition to these washers, there is also a timber connector, which can be used between pieces of wood that which are being bolted together to prevent slipping.

Bolts for Fixing Wood to Hard Surfaces

Rag
This has a jagged head, which is set in concrete with the thread protruding upwards so that wood or metal may be attached.

Anchor
Available in various sizes and ideal for fixing to concrete or wood. It is essential that the hole is drilled slightly larger than the anchor base so that when the bolt is tightened, the expansion arms and grip tips on the bolt open to give excellent holding power.

Glue

Woodworking adhesive is not widely used when working outside, although it is essential when fixing woodworking joints together, and therefore it is important that waterproof glue is used. All parts of the joint must fit quite well together as wood adhesive does not fill gaps easily although it can be mixed with powder filler where joints are uneven

TOOLS AND THEIR USES

Excavation Tools

When building wooden structures such as sheds, decking and fencing, it is imperative that the correct tools are used for the groundwork operations to ensure that the work is carried out correctly, safely and with the minimum amount of effort, therefore the following tools should be considered:

Spades
The best type to use for general excavation work is a contractor's spade, which has a longer and thinner head than the garden spade, making it perfect for digging heavy, sticky and difficult to penetrate materials such as clay.

Shovels
There are many types of shovels that can be used for different operations. These include:

- Round-mouth shovel. Very useful for moving loose materials such as ballast but is also good for digging close to plants without uprooting them.

- Square and taper-mouth shovels. The ideal choice when it comes to shovelling out, backfilling or spreading.
- Trenching, drainage and cable-laying shovels. These have narrow and slightly tapered blades, which make them the preferred choice for trenching, post holes and footings.

Forks

For general excavation work, which involves the breaking up of heavy clay or stony ground, a contractor's fork should be used, which has chisel point prongs and is wider, with longer prongs than a garden fork.

Double-Handled Shovel Holers

Used for digging post holes, especially where extra depth is required.

Crowbars

Essential for breaking up hard ground – especially useful for preparing guide holes before hammering in fence posts.

Tampers

Ideal for firming material around posts, and so on.

Pickaxes and Mattocks

Pickaxes are generally used to break up stony or hard ground, whereas mattocks are best suited for heavy ground, especially where there are tree roots.

Hand Tools

Saws

Saws come in all shapes and sizes, and their uses can be determined by their ppi (number of teeth per inch). The saws with fewer teeth are best for softwoods whilst saws with greater numbers of

A trenching shovel.

A double-handled shovel holer.

A large tamper that can be used for firming ground and around posts.

teeth are used for cutting hardwoods. There are basically four types of handsaws used in timber construction:

- The crosscut saw, which is 60–66cm (24–26in) in length with 6–8ppi, is used for cutting across the grain on both softwood and hardwood and also for working with the grain when dealing with the tougher hardwoods.
- The ripsaw is 66cm (26in) long with 5ppi and is the right choice for cutting softwoods along the grain.
- The panel saw is 50–55cm (20in–22in) in length, with 10ppi. It is mainly used for fine cross-cut and jointing work and also for cutting sheet wood materials.
- The tenon saw is 20–35cm (8–14in) in length with 13–20ppi and is used for cutting smaller pieces of wood when cutting across the grain and jointing.

Screwdrivers

There are two main types of screwdriver – straight thread and cross-slot. Screw head sizes vary so it is best to purchase a ratchet-type screwdriver with interchangeable heads or a boxed set that includes a selection of small, medium and large-headed screwdrivers that will suit a variety of jobs. However, a 6mm (¼in) slot and cross-head screwdriver will fit a wide range of screws used in wooden structure construction.

This 42-piece socket set, has enough sockets to cover a wide range of bolt head sizes.

Socket Sets

A socket set is required for securing types of bolts and one should be chosen with the correct-sized sockets for the bolts you are using.

Spanners

A set of open-ended spanners is generally required when using nuts and bolts to attach wood to wood. They are normally used to hold the nut secure whilst you tighten up the bolt with the socket set, but are also useful in situations where it is difficult to access the bolts with a socket set.

Hammers

The main type of hammer used in woodworking is the claw hammer, which usually weighs 450–570g (16–24oz), and is used for both driving in nails and removing them. However, for more delicate work, and where smaller nails are used, the pin hammer is the best choice as its wedge-shaped end is ideal for starting small nails whilst holding them in position with your fingers.

Chisels

It is not essential to have a full set of chisels – a 6mm (¼in) and an 18mm (¾in) bevelled-edge chisel will suffice in most cases. These types of chisels are bevelled for a purpose – using them flat side down allows you to dig as deep into the wood as you want. Alternatively, by using them the other way round, the bevel prevents the chisel going deeper. It is essential that chisels are regularly sharpened and always cleaned and lightly oiled after use.

Spirit Levels

There are many different types of spirit levels. The most widely used is the box- section type, which has one horizontal and one vertical vial. This is used when levelling hard surfaces in readiness for erecting a wooden structure, or checking the horizontal and vertical levels of the structure itself. They usually come in four lengths: 30cm (12in), 60cm (24in), 90cm (3ft), and 120cm (4ft). The size of spirit level required depends on what type of structure is being constructed, however a 60cm (24in) level will normally suffice for most purposes.

As well as the conventional type of level, the post

level is an essential tool in wood construction. It has a hinged body that opens, and can be used both on square and round timber. There are straps that can attach it to the timber, which makes it ideal when working on your and has two horizontal and one diagonal vials, so that the level of both upright and cross-timbers can be checked, or it can be used to check the vertical and horizontal levels at the same time, for example when putting in posts.

Measures

For general use, a 5m (16ft) tape measure is big enough for most jobs, although larger sizes are available. A 60cm (24in) steel tape measure is ideal for drawing lines between measured points and for more intricate measuring.

Try Squares

Essential for checking that the wood is square and also for marking lines at right angles. A 20cm (8in) or 23cm (9in) try square is the most useful size as it is long enough to cover most wood sizes and can also be used without difficulty on narrower wood.

It is advisable to check a new try square, and an old one occasionally, by holding it in position against a piece of wood with a straight edge and drawing a line against the blade, then reversing it so that it is against the opposite straight edge of the wood. Check that the drawn line follows the blade's edge. If it does not, then the try square is faulty and should be replaced.

Mitre Blocks

These are used to cut 45-degree angles on the ends of timber so when they are secured to each other they form a 90-degree angle, which is required when making wooden structures such as gates.

Workbenches

Invaluable when it comes to woodworking, the workbench is fitted with a vice, which allows you to hold the timber in place whilst working on it, be it to chisel out for a joint or to cut it to size.

Power Tools

Hand-held power tools play an important role in modern construction and are available as corded

A post level being used to check a post.

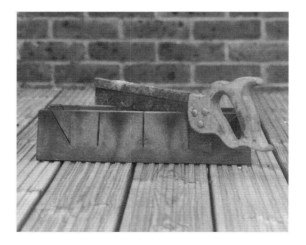

A mitre block and mitre saw.

31

A mobile folding workbench.

and cordless models. However, for versatility when it comes to outside construction, the best choice is probably the cordless model, as you can use it anywhere without the need of a power source, it is relatively lightweight, and can be used in wet weather.

One of the most frequently asked questions with cordless equipment is – how long will the battery last? The answer to this is that it all depends on what is being drilled, the frequency of use, temperature, and whether the battery is at full charge. Probably the best way to ensure that a power tool has enough charge for the day is to have a couple of spare batteries on standby that are fully charged up. The time required to charge a battery pack depends on the type of battery and charger, and can vary from one hour to overnight. A general rule for recharging batteries is to do it when the drop in performance is noticeable, not when the tool stops working, as this may shorten the life of the battery. Most cordless equipment comes with 2AH batteries, which are fine for average use. However, if high power and constant use is required, it is worth investing in 3AH battery packs.

The power tools that prove invaluable in most wood construction situations are as follows:

Drills

Cordless equipment is measured in volts – the higher the voltage, the more powerful the tool. Cordless drills usually have a voltage of 9.6–24v. However the higher the voltage, the heavier the drill will be. For average use, a drill of about 14.4v weighing about 1.8–2kg (4–5lb) is sufficient.

Choose a reversible drill, as this is essential when using screwdriver bits. Other features to look for in a drill include variable speed, as this allows you to control the bit speed, which is necessary when using such attachments as sanding discs and also when

A cordless drill.

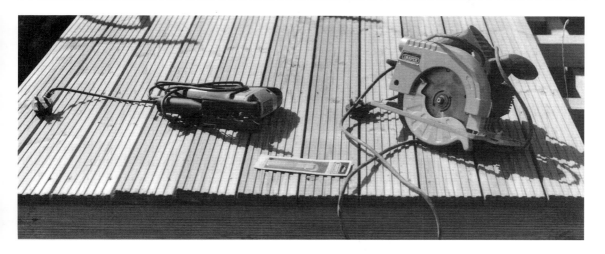

A corded circular saw and jig saw.

working on different types of surfaces. An adjustable clutch setting is a must as the clutch reacts to the resistance of the material being drilled or to the screw itself if being used as a screwdriver, which allows holes to be drilled of a consistent depth and prevents you from driving screws too deep and snapping a screw or stripping a screw head. As well as the variable speed and adjustable clutch, it is also worth considering purchasing a drill with a hammer setting as this helps you to drill deeply and precisely into hardwood or masonry.

As stated, a cordless drill will suit the majority of your needs when constructing wooden structures. However, when drilling into masonry or drilling large in wood, it may be worth considering using a corded model as this type of work will run the battery down quickly.

Screwdrivers and Impact Drivers

Cordless screwdrivers are usually 2v and are the preferred option for odd jobs around the house and for the constant screwing and unscrewing on a wooden structure. On the other hand, an impact driver is best for heavy-duty work – it hits the screw or bolt hundreds of times to blast it into wood and is ideal for constructing decking or any other structure where many screws or bolts are used.

Saws

The two main types of saws used are the jig saw and the circular saw. The jig saw is the more versatile of the two as it allows you to cut wood in different shapes and combines the functions of a band and a scroll saw. The circular saw is mainly used for cutting wood to size. They are both available as cordless models, which are ideal in situations where corded models are difficult to use, although continuous use can drain the battery fairly quickly. In situations where there is no power source, it is recommended that the majority of the cutting work is carried out in another location, leaving just the finishing touches to be completed on site.

Other Power Tools

The power tools previously described are probably the main ones you will require for the majority of outdoor wooden structure projects, although for larger or more intricate projects other power tools may be required, such as power nailers, sanders or routers.

CHAPTER 3

Sheds, Storage Units, Summerhouses and Playhouses

CHOOSING AND PREPARING THE SITE

Once you have decided what type of building you are going to construct and what purpose it is going to be used for, the next decision concerns which way it is going to face.

North Facing

By facing your building towards the north, you will get the morning sun but during the winter months it can get very cold and therefore insulation and effective heating is required if it is going to be used throughout the year. However, a north-facing structure will make an ideal storage area, as it will remain cool even during hot weather, so that many different types of materials can be stored without the risk of overheating.

South Facing

This type of structure will get sunshine all day long and therefore in the summer months it will get very hot, which makes this type of situation ideal for a summerhouse or gazebo. However, the installation of blinds or ventilation may be advisable to prevent overheating.

East Facing

An east-facing structure will benefit from the early morning sun, which will provide heat to the structure and by insulating the building you can prevent the warmth escaping. This situation is ideal for a shed that is to be used as a workshop, although there is a risk of it becoming too warm, especially in the summer.

West Facing

This is another aspect that will get very warm during the day and will also catch the evening sun. Ideal for relaxing outside, especially where evening use is also required

SIZE OF THE STRUCTURE

Before beginning to design the type of structure you wish to build or purchase, it is important to work out what size is needed. This depends to some extent on its intended use, but more importantly it is governed by the amount of land available. The proposed site should be surveyed and any structural features, such as manhole covers and drainage pipes, need to be identified and put on a plan as these may need to be relocated.

It is also good practice where possible to try to position any structure at least 1m (3ft 4in) away from any other structures such as buildings or fences. The reason for this being that it allows room for installation and will facilitate effective future maintenance. The location of trees should also be noted because, if situated too close, the longevity of the structure could be affected and more maintenance required.

Once the size and location has been decided upon, the area can be marked out. The best way to do this is by using string and pegs. Once this has been done,

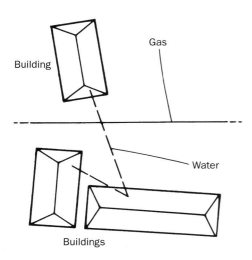

Services marked on the plan.

you need to stand back and look at the site, to ensure that the size of the structure will not only suit the purpose it is to be used for, but also that it will fit into the area. If either of these criteria is not met, the pegs and lines can be altered until the desired effect is achieved.

The height of the structure should also be noted, as the location of any overhead services needs to be considered.

SERVICES

The services required will depend on the type of structure and how it is to be used. When deciding where to position your new structure, the location of mains services needs to be ascertained. As a general rule, the closer to the main building the proposed structure is situated, the easier it will be to supply electricity, water, and so on. If it is any distance away from an existing building, it is advisable to get quotes from professional contractors for laying on these services prior to commencement of any works. The types of services that may need to be considered include electricity, gas, sewerage, drains, telephone lines and water.

CONSTRUCTING A BASE

It is essential that a firm, level and square base is made before any structure is constructed. If this is not provided, the building will be unstable and unfit for use. In order to ensure your chosen type of base is

Marking out the site using string and pegs.

square, the 3–4–5 method of marking out should be adopted, which entails driving a small square stake into a corner where you intend the base to begin. Once this has been done, measure 90cm (3ft) along the width of the base, and 1.2m (4ft) lengthwise, and then mark these points with canes. Finally, measure between the two caned points to form a triangle. This measurement should be 1.5m (5ft); if this measurement is not correct then one of the canes should be moved until the correct reading is obtained. By undertaking this procedure, it ensures that the corner will be at a 90-degree angle. Once the first corner is correct, a measurement can be taken to each of the other corners, and the 3–4–5 method used again, to ensure that the base is square. Alternatively, wooden set squares can be constructed and used to produce the same result.

After this has been done, you can decide which type of base you require, choosing from one of the following.

Concrete

This is the best method for any building that is greater than 29sqm (312sq ft), for a garage or summerhouse, a building with no suspended wooden floor, or any type of building that will be in continual use. However, it is essential that the base is constructed correctly. The thickness of concrete for the average garden shed is 7.5cm (3in). However, for larger structures, or on softer ground, 10cm (4in) of concrete is required. In both of these cases, 5cm (2in) of hardcore should be laid and compacted. Once the depth of the footings has been decided, mark out the area and dig out to the required depth. The formwork should then be put into position. The timber should be as deep as the footings and held in place by wooden pegs.

With larger bases it will be necessary to lay the concrete in sections with expansion joints laid between each of the sections because the larger the slab of concrete, the more chance there is of it cracking. The contraction joints are best made from treated 2.5cm (1in) thick softwood as deep as the framework and long enough to fit across the inside. They should be held in place by wooden pegs. The distance between the contraction joints varies according to the depth of the concrete and site width, and the joints should be closer as the width gets narrower. As a general guideline the following rules apply:

- For a base with a width of 2.4–3m (8–10ft), the contraction joints should be placed at 3m (10ft) intervals for a 7.5cm (3in) thick base, whereas if the concrete is laid to a depth of 10cm (4in), the contraction joints can be laid slightly further apart at 4m (13ft) intervals.

Squaring the base using wooden set squares.

A concrete footing within a timber frame, held in position by wooden pegs.

- If the base width is slightly narrower, for example 1–2m (3ft 4in–7ft), then for a base 7.5cm (3in) thick, the contraction joints should be 1.8m (6ft) apart, with the contraction joints for a 10cm (4in) thick base being 1.8–3m (6–10ft) apart.

The mix for concrete is 1:5 parts cement to ballast, which can be either measured using a bucket for accuracy, or by the traditional method of level shovelfuls. It is best to use a cement mixer for large quantities of concrete, and water should be added gradually until the mix is uniform in colour and workable. It is very important that the mix is not too wet as this will weaken the concrete.

The correct way to lay concrete is to place a layer at the bottom of the framework and then compact it down with a rammer, ensuring that the concrete is pushed into the corners. The sides of the edges of the framework should be tapped as the concrete is laid, so that a solid edge is formed. Layers of concrete should be laid one on top of one another until the concrete reaches the top of the timber. When the final layer is put in place it should be firmed down using a tamping board. A chopping and sawing motion should be used, working from one end of the framework to the other. After tamping down the concrete, it will be necessary to smooth it out with a float if it is intended that the structure is to have a wooden floor. If the area is smoothed out, this will allow the batons of the floor to sit evenly. It is also

important that the concrete does not dry out too quickly. Therefore, when you are laying concrete and the weather is warm, you should cover it with plastic sheeting until it has hardened off. You should then spray the surface with water to prevent it cracking.

Another problem with wet concrete is frost damage. This can be prevented by adding a frost prevention additive that can be purchased from most DIY stores or builder's merchants. Frost protection additives speed up the reaction between water and cement, which reduces the risk of frost damage whilst the mix is wet, but it is also important that the concrete is covered with plastic sheeting for three days in order to protect it.

Slab

This is an easier and cheaper alternative to a concrete base. However, it is important that the slabs are laid correctly and this involves good ground preparation. Without it, the structure will become unstable. Slab bases are not always the best option where there is constant or heavy use and they are also unsuitable for larger structures. However, paving slabs can be useful in situations where the structure is not going to be permanent or in cases where it will be moved in future years.

The depth and preparation of the base on which the slabs are going to be laid varies according to the actual weight and use of the structure, and is also dependent on the nature of the ground. However, as

The slabs need to be completely level, ready for the shed base.

a general guideline, 10cm (4in) of compacted hard-core should be laid to form a firm base. This should then be topped with approximately 6.5cm (2½in) of sharp sand, or grit, with cement mixed into the sand. The mixture should equate to 5:1 parts sand to cement. The mixture should be compacted to 5cm (2in), and you should ensure that the surface is level. The slabs should be laid by bedding the first slab into position at one corner. The level can then be taken off this slab in all directions using a spirit level. It is very important that all the slabs are absolutely level with the first slab, otherwise the whole base will be 'out'.

If a slab is too high, it can be gently tapped with a rubber mallet across the offending edge until it is in line. Alternatively, if a slab is too low, it should be lifted and a small amount of the dry mix of the sand and cement placed beneath it until it reaches the correct level. If the slab will not bed down properly, lift it and continue to remove a little sand at a time until it reaches the correct level.

Timber Bearers

This is the simplest solution. However, it is not suitable for all types of buildings – for example, any structure that is greater than 29sq m (312sq ft), a corner unit, a gazebo, a garage, or a building with no suspended floor.

This type of base can be placed straight onto the earth, as long as the ground is level and firm;

although the ideal method is to place the bearers onto slabs. Where the ground is prone to waterlogging, it is a good idea to lay a 5cm (2in) layer of pea shingle on top, which will allow good drainage. This is ideal for damp sites, because it raises the building off the ground, which stops any damp from rising and allows good air circulation underneath the structure. The timber bearers, which will have been pressure treated, should measure 7.5×5cm (3×2in) and be spaced evenly apart. They should be laid lengthwise – the exact spacing will depend on the size of the base. Alternatively, railway sleepers can be used as bearers. However, if this method is adopted it should be noted that a step or ramp may be required for access as the sleepers will raise it further off the ground.

TYPES OF WOODEN BUILDINGS

Sheds

Sheds are primarily functional buildings, usually with one or more windows. They can be used as work-shops, for general storage, potting-up plants and a variety of other activities.

Storage Units

Storage units are purpose-built structures used to store tools, equipment, coal, and any other items that need to be made secure and protected from the elements. Storage units are usually much smaller than sheds – often too small to allow a person to actually

A shed laid on timber bearers.

A shed laid on sleepers.

A large, newly constructed shed in a children's playground. All the windows are on the side nearest to the grass banking to avoid damage from ball games.

A storage unit with double doors for easy access.

A chalet-type summerhouse.

A children's playhouse.

A children's tree house.

enter them, making them ideal for smaller gardens or areas where a shed would be too obtrusive.

Summerhouses

Similar to a conservatory in that they can be used as an extension to the living space and as places to relax and view the garden. Summerhouses are usually decorative structures, forming a feature of the garden that also has a functional purpose. There are basically two types of summerhouses.

Extensively Glazed

This offers a protected environment for relaxation and viewing the garden. However, because of the extensive glazing, this type of summerhouse can be very warm in the summer months.

Chalet-Type

Provides an additional living area. Because it has fewer windows, it can also be used for hobbies and other recreational purposes. It often has a veranda to provide additional protection from the sun.

Playhouses

Playhouses, which are miniature versions of summer-houses, make an ideal play area for younger children. Unfortunately, children can soon outgrow them – especially the more basic structures. However, in some situations they can also double as storage areas for items of play equipment.

Tree Houses

Tree houses are basically playhouses in the sky, and the best trees to build them in are oak, fir, hemlock, and maple although they can also be constructed quite safely in apple, pine, elm, and willow trees. The tree should not be rotting or diseased and the load-bearing branches must be sound and a minimum of 15cm (6in) in diameter. The most suitable shape is where the branches resemble an open hand, or cradle.

The actual shape and design of the structure can only decided after the precise location has been finalized. The platform needs to be secured to the tree. When doing this, do not use copper fittings or cut and remove bark more than halfway around the trunk as this will kill the tree.

Safety is always of paramount importance when constructing any raised structure, and building regulations require that railings are fitted to any platform that is more than 46cm (18in) off the ground.

SELF-ASSEMBLY WOODEN BUILDINGS

There is now a wide range of good quality, purpose-built wooden buildings available, which can be erected by either the supplier or a contractor, or are available in kit form for self-assembly. The advantages in choosing this type of building are as follows:

- They are readily available and you can usually visit a show area and see exactly what types of wooden buildings are available.
- The pricing structure is fixed, making budgeting easier.
- The kits are complete and usually come with full instructions for ease of assembly.

Their main disadvantage is that the sizes and styles available may not be exactly what you require, although there are ways to customize your building by adding features or altering the overall appearance.

Self-assembly kits usually these come with their own instructions and assembly methods will differ according to the structure being erected. The following directions are offered as a guideline only as, where possible, the manufacturer's instructions should always be referred to and followed when erecting any type of self-assembly structure. However, they may be useful in situations where there are no instructions, such as with second-hand buildings, or where the instructions are hard to follow or unclear. It should also be noted that these instructions refer to the erection of apex sheds, although the same rules apply when erecting pent-roof buildings and some reference is made to these.

Selecting a Self-Assembly Wooden Building

Once you have decided to purchase a self-assembly model and established what type of building you require, the next step is to select a structure that will not only fit into your budget but will also meet your functional requirements. You also need to ensure that it is manufactured to a standard that will guarantee reasonable longevity. If possible, it is best to visit a show site where you can see the buildings erected and

look at the kits themselves. The following points should be considered.

Cladding
There are different types of cladding available and the cheaper sheds tend to be clad with feather- or waney-edged weatherboarding. Unfortunately, this is not the strongest type of cladding available, or the most weatherproof. If the structure is to be sited in a more open position, it may be better to choose a building with tongue-and-groove, shiplap, or barrelled cladding – similar to shiplap but gives a log cabin effect. These are stronger and will cope with extreme weather better. If softwood cladding has been used, this should have been pressure treated and the boards free from cracks and extensive knot holes.

Doors
The width of the door is an important factor to consider. If, for example, the building is to be used for storing garden equipment, it has to be wide enough to allow easy access for mowers and other types of machinery. If a solid door is chosen, this should be of a strong construction with at least three ledges and two braces. A strong lock is essential for security purposes and all metal parts should be rust-proof.

Eaves
There need to be sufficient overhangs to protect the walls from rainfall.

Floors
Tongue-and-groove boards create the best visual effect and will last longer than both plywood and hardwood, but they are more expensive.

Framework
When looking in the shed, the beams that form the upright framework should be no more than 60cm (24in) apart and there should be cross-beams between them to prevent the building from bowing and provide additional strength.

Roofing
Always go inside the building and check that there is sufficient headroom. If the budget allows for, it opt

Three different types of cladding.

Tongue-and-groove.

Feather-edge.

Shiplap.

for a tongue-and-groove board roof rather than a plywood one. If the roofing felt supplied with the shed is not a heavy-grade material, it may be worthwhile to purchase heavy-grade fibre-based roofing felt. This will reduce maintenance costs in the long term and ensure a watertight building for a much longer period. It should also be noted when purchasing roofing felt, or if it is supplied with the structure, that there should be enough to cover under the eave beams otherwise there will be a weak spot where the felt may lift, allowing water to leak through the roof.

Windows

The number of windows required is ultimately determined by the intended use of the building. For example, with a small general-purpose shed, one window will usually be sufficient. However, if the area is to be used predominately for recreational or work purposes, you will need at least one window that can be opened to provide ventilation. In the case of summerhouses, generally, the more windows you have, the better, because this makes for better viewing of the garden, allows the building to warm naturally during the summer months, and gives the inside of the building a light and airy feel. In some cases, you may need to look at the glazing materials supplied. This is particularly important for structures such as playhouses where you may wish to opt for a

polycarbonate material, which is safer. Even with summerhouses, especially in gardens where there are children, it is advisable to opt for safety glass.

Erecting a Self-Assembly Wooden Building

Erecting any type of wooden building is usually a two-person operation, otherwise it will difficult to put up the side panels and the roof sections. The following instructions are intended as a guide only, as parts of the shed may differ as could some of the construction details. Any manufacturer's instructions that come with the shed should be referred to and followed.

Before starting to assemble the shed, it is a good idea to apply an additional coat of wood preservative to the underside of the floor; as once the shed has been erected, this area will be inaccessible for future maintenance. Once the preservative has dried, the floor should be placed onto the prepared base. As a general rule, even on a concrete or slab base, it is best to use bearers as these will help with air circulation and prevent damp rising through the floor, thus prolonging the life of the shed.

The floor should be checked to ensure it is level and then the back panel and one side panel can be put into position with the lip on the panels overhanging the floor. The panels should be checked to ensure that they are level and that they will nail

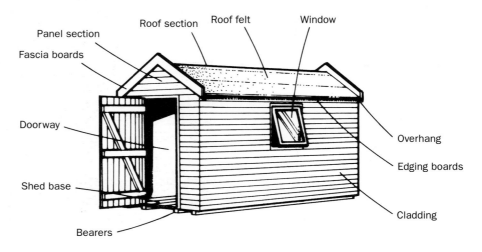

The components of a shed.

together. As a general rule, 5cm (2in) nails should be used when fixing the side panels together and attaching the roof sections. When nailing to the bearers, a longer nail is usually required – a 7.5cm (3in) nail will usually suffice. After the two panels have been nailed together and attached to the floor, they should be made more stable by nailing the bottom rails of the panels into the bearers. Fit the remaining panels in the same way and then check once more that the building is level.

The next step is to fit the two roof sections. It is important that there is equal overhang along the edge of the shed, and in the case of apex sheds, that this overhang is equal on both the front and rear and that they slot into position. Some shed designs have cut-outs in the front and rear gables, lightly nailed into position. In this case, the second roof section should be put in place, ensuring that it is in line with the first. If the roof sections are not square this means that the shed base has moved and it is not level. If this is the case, lift one of the corners until you get the correct level and then place some packing under it. Once this has been done, nail through the centre batons of the roof to join them together and then nail through the roof at 5cm (2in) intervals into the side panels.

Now that the roof is in position, you need to felt the shed. This is done by cutting the felt to size, bearing in mind that there needs to be 6.5cm (2½in) overhang on each edge which means that each piece needs to be 13cm (5in) longer than the roof.

Secure with tacks, starting at the bottom edge of the roof and ensuring that the felt remains flat. It should be bent over the edges at right angles and cut at the corners to give a neat finish. The tacks should be put in approximately 15cm (6in) apart when nailing into the roof. If you have to remove any tacks because they have not gone in correctly, any damage should be covered with mastic to ensure a watertight finish. Each piece of felt should overlap the adjoining piece, and on apex sheds the final piece of felt should be placed over the ridge.

Once all the felt has been laid, the fascia and edging boards should be nailed into position. To complete the shed, the windows should be glazed and doors hung. The glass panels are put into position and then held in place by using glazing beads, which

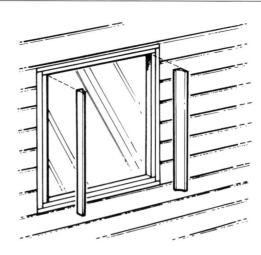

Glazing beads holding the glass in place.

are usually thin pieces of wood held by small nails and supplied as part of the kit. For the door, use three hinges with 2.5cm (1in) screws, making sure that they are square and level with each other at equal distance from the top and bottom – usually 20–25cm (8–10in), and one positioned in the middle of the door. The door should be positioned in the opening

A double door, hung using three hinges on each door, spaced evenly apart.

A living, mixed sedum roof.

as high as possible with equal spacing either side. To hold the hinges in place on the frame, a single nail can be driven into both the top and bottom hinges and screwed into position. Once this has been done, the middle hinge can be fitted.

Customizing a Self-Assembly Wooden Building

Although self-assembly wooden buildings are based on the most popular designs and are mass-produced, there are ways in which these buildings can be customized to make them unique.

The Living Roof

Living, or green roofs as they are sometimes known, originate from Scandinavia, where traditionally turf was laid on roofs to help protect and insulate them.

Modern green roofs are primarily made from sedum because as well as acting as an insulator they also have an attractive, all year round, appearance.

In order to construct a living roof you need to line the roof with heavy-duty plastic sheeting on top of the roofing felt. It is best to use a whole sheet so that there is less chance of water leaking through. It should be pulled tight and nailed along the edges with roofing tacks. If plastic sheeting is not used, the sedum could be poisoned by being in direct contact with the roofing felt. Moreover, the excessive dampness may cause the felt to deteriorate and the roof to leak.

Edging boards need to be attached to the sides and edges of the roof to a 5cm (2in) depth to form a frame to contain the growing medium. The best type of medium to use is equal parts of vermiculite and perlite. This lightweight mixture of sterile minerals has excellent water retention qualities and retains heat, which insulates the roof and keeps the plant roots warm. Also, because the solution is sterile there is less chance that it will harbour pests and diseases that can damage the sedum. It is best to mix the vermiculite and perlite with water so that it forms a pliable mixture. Start at the bottom of the roof, and firm it with a wooden board so that the mixture lies just below the edging board and work your way up the roof, levelling and firming at the same time.

The sedum used for roofing is usually supplied in rolls similar to turf. On apex sheds, start laying the rolls so that they sit evenly over the ridge of the shed and firm down as you lay them. Once the entire roof has been covered, stretch plastic-coated chicken wire over the entire surface to hold the sedum in position. The wire can be secured by stapling it to the edging boards.

The roof should then be 'watered in'. It is

important to continue to water it in dry weather, as the sedum should not be allowed to dry out. The roof should not be watered when there is direct sunlight as this will damage the sedum – as a general rule, early morning and evening watering is best.

Imitation Thatch

An imitation thatch roof can be created by using woven reed fencing rolls. These are for decorative purposes only, and should be laid over a felt roof. The woven reed should be laid evenly over the ridge of an apex shed from the top downwards, and placed in position by stapling the wire framework to the roof.

Shingles

Cedar and oak shingles are used to give a rustic feel to a timber building, although asphalt shingles can be used to give a tiled roofing effect, and they are a lot cheaper. To ensure that the roof is watertight, it is best to lay a layer of roofing felt first then the shingles can be laid on top of this. You should work from the eaves upwards and the shingles should overhang the eave slightly. The shingles in the rows should be butted up to each other and nailed along the top edge, with each row overhanging the row in front of it so that the nailed part of the shingle is not visible. The rows should be staggered, and it is a good idea to lay a board in front of the shingles as they are laid to ensure that the rows are straight.

A chain drain attached to the corner of the roof.

Chain Drains

Chain drains not only improve the visual aspect of a building, but also have a practical purpose in that they can be used to drain surface water off the roof and into barrels, which then can be used in the garden.

The chains are attached to each of the four corners of the roof and drain the water into barrels situated below them. Holes are drilled in each of the four corners of the roof; the chains are threaded through these holes and then secured to the surface of the roof. In order to direct the water towards the chains, the edging boards should protrude approximately 2.5cm (1in) above the surface, and then either a small plastic gully or sheeting can be attached to the inside of the boards.

Colour Enhancement

Another way to customize your shed or summer-house, which will make it compatible with your surroundings, and also give it an individuality of its own is to apply a wood stain, which is widely available in a range of colours. It is best to apply a water-based wood stain. Unlike many paints and varnishes, this will stain, waterproof and protect the timber by

Examples of oak shingles.

preventing water from entering and evaporating inside the wood, thus enabling it to breath and preventing the surface from cracking, peeling and blistering. The wood stain also highlights both the grain of the timber and the natural beauty of the entire structure.

Insulation

If a wooden building is regularly used for recreational and work purposes, it should be insulated to reduce draughts and the risk of frost. This is especially important if it is being used to over-winter plant material such as dahlia tubers. By insulating, you will also reduce the risk of rust forming on machinery and tools. The best and easiest way is to cut some rigid, expanded polystyrene sheets to size and nail these between the frames. Once this has been done, tempered-grade hardwood or external-grade plywood should be nailed to the frames to protect the polystyrene and enhance the appearance of the interior.

Additional Features

In order to further enhance the appearance of wooden buildings, a range of other features can also be added, including ornamental window shutters, window boxes, ornate fascia boards, or even a decking area with a banister surround, which not only enhances the appearance of the building but has a functional purpose as well.

An example of invasive climbers, which should be avoided.

Use of Plants

Trellis panels can be attached to the walls of the building and climbers planted that will grow along it. However, it is important to choose non-invasive climbers, such as roses, which can be controlled by pruning and can be untied and removed from the trellis in the winter months to allow maintenance work.

BUILDING A WOODEN STRUCTURE TO YOUR OWN DESIGN

You can design and construct your building completely from scratch, but this is not to be recommended for the beginner, or anyone with little experience in designing or building wooden structures.

Plans for wooden buildings are readily available to buy off the Internet. These give the basic dimensions and construction details for many different types of wooden structures, including sheds, storage areas, summerhouses, gazebos and playhouses. These form a good base for designing and constructing your wooden structure. The sizes can be altered to suit the particular space available. The disadvantage, as with the ready-made structures, is that by purchasing plans you are limited to certain types of designs. However, you can use the plans as a template and alter them to your own design.

Construction Methods

There are basically three types of construction methods used and these are as follows.

Pole Framing

This is the oldest method used in the construction of wooden buildings and can be dated back to the Stone Age. Recently this method has come back into favour, mainly because it is fairly simple to construct at a relatively low cost. Moreover, pressurized poles have become more readily available. This is especially important in this construction method because the poles are usually set into concrete in the ground, or onto concrete piers or footings, and the fact that the timber poles have been pressure treated means that the life of the building is prolonged. This type of construction is ideal in remote, isolated situations

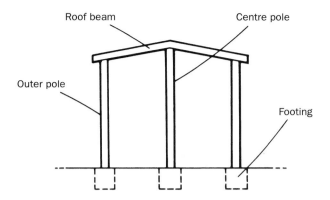

Pole framing.

where it is difficult to prepare a firm base and it may also be used in situations where rapid construction is required.

Post and Beam Framing
This method dates back to medieval times. Post and beam framing is a heavy-duty type of construction, built on a concrete base. The beams and posts that form the frame measure either 15cm (6in), or 20cm (8in) square. This is a fairly expensive method and requires some skill; however it does have the advantages of being strong, durable and more fire resistant

than smaller post and beam buildings. In addition, the strength of these structures allows the use of larger doors and windows.

Stud Framing
There are two types of stud framing: platform and balloon.

- **Platform framing**. This is the most common modern method and is widely used in the construction of smaller wooden buildings. The timbers for this type of structure range

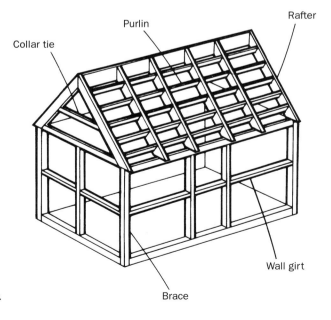

Post and beam framing.

49

in size from 50mm (2in)×100mm (4in) to 50mm (2in)×300mm (6in), and are regularly spaced to form walls, floors and roofs. The construction methods are simpler than those for post and beam framing, less labour intensive, and involve fewer materials. In fact, the materials are so light that it is possible for one person to construct this type of frame

- **Balloon framing**. This does not tend to be commonly used but it is one way of framing a two-storey building. The main difference between this type of framing and platform framing is that the studs run continuously from the base to the top and the floors are held on supports attached to the studs.

CONSTRUCTION PLANS, MATERIALS AND INSTRUCTIONS

The following plan is for a basic 2.4×3m (8×10ft) apex shed with a single door and window that can either be used as it is or adapted for other applications.

Materials

It is recommended that the wood used for this construction is pressure-treated softwood, and listed below are the material requirements for the shed.

Floor Framework
Two pieces of 3m (10ft), 15×5cm (6×2in) softwood
Six pieces of 2.4m (8ft), 15×5cm (6×2in) softwood

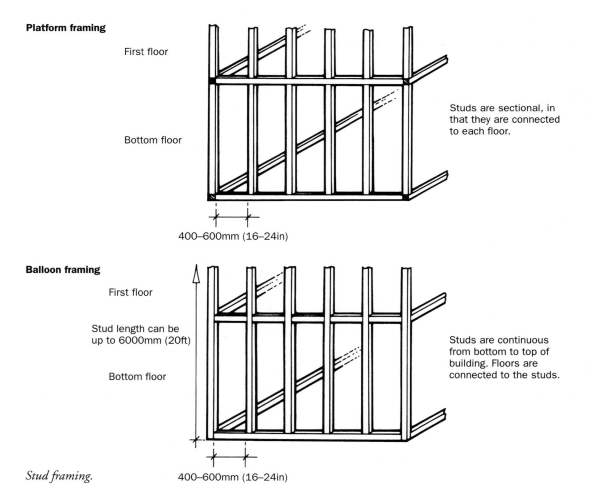

Platform framing

First floor

Bottom floor

Studs are sectional, in that they are connected to each floor.

400–600mm (16–24in)

Balloon framing

First floor

Stud length can be up to 6000mm (20ft)

Bottom floor

Studs are continuous from bottom to top of building. Floors are connected to the studs.

Stud framing.

400–600mm (16–24in)

Bearers
Four pieces of 3m×10cm (10ft×6in), softwood

Flooring
Three sheets of 19mm (¾in), 2.4×1.2m (8×4ft) plywood

Main Framework
Twenty-six pieces of 2.4 (8ft), 10×5cm (4×2in) softwood
Four pieces of 2.4m (8ft), 10×5cm (4×2in) softwood

Beam Supports and Rafters
Twelve pieces of 2.7m (9ft), 10×5cm (4×2in) softwood
One piece of 3m (10ft), 10×5cm (4×2in) softwood
Four pieces of 35cm (14in), 10×5cm (4×2in) softwood
Two pieces of 28cm (11in), 10×5cm (4×2in) softwood

Roof
Four sheets of 12mm (½in), 2.4×1.2m (8×4ft) plywood

Cladding
Types of cladding include:

• Barrelled (log effect)
• Feather-edged
• Shiplap
• Tongue-and-groove
• Waney-edged

The amount required depends on the choice of cladding, and a timber merchant should be consulted to determine the exact quantity.

Roofing Material
10sqm (100sq ft) of heavy-grade fibre-based roofing felt

Eave and Fascia Boards
18m (60ft) of 15×2.5cm (6×1in) softwood

Doors
The size of door depends on what the shed is to be used for but it is important to note that the frame must be 10mm (½in) higher and wider than the door.

Windows
The size of the window can vary but it must fit in the available space and therefore it is essential that these measurements are finalized before construction begins.

Construction Detail
When constructing this type of structure, it is recommended that it is undertaken with the aid of another person.

Floor Framework
Construct a basic oblong frame by nailing together the two 3m (10ft) joists and two of the 2.4m (8ft) joists. Once this has been done, position and nail the four remaining 2.4m (8ft) joists spaced at 60cm (24in) intervals in the centre of the framework.

Bearers
Nail two of the 3m (10ft) bearers to the underside of the framework, 30cm (12in) in from the outer edge. Once this has been done, the two remaining bearers should be spaced evenly between the two outer bearers and nailed in position.

Flooring
The plywood sheeting should be cut to size so that it can be securely nailed to the joists.

Main Framework, Beam Supports and Rafters
First, construct the four basic frames for the walls using the same construction techniques as for the floor framework. The dimensions for these frames are 2 × 2400mm square and 2 × 2400×3000mm. The interior joists for the frames can now be put into position for one of the side panels and the back panel. These joists should be spaced at 60cm (24in) intervals and nailed in position.

The other two panels should be made up to accommodate the door and window – for the dimensions and spacing of the joists for these sections, please refer to the diagrams on page 53.

The next step is to nail the panels together and attach them to the constructed wooden floor. Once this has been done it is time to concentrate on the

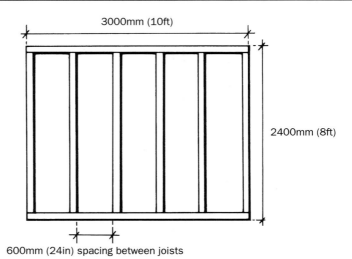

3000mm (10ft)

2400mm (8ft)

Floor framework.

600mm (24in) spacing between joists

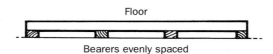

Floor

Positioning the bearers.

Bearers evenly spaced

roof. First, you need to make up the beam supports from the four lengths of timber measuring 35cm (14in) and two pieces of 28cm (12in). These can then be joined together and attached to the erected side framework to form the initial roof frame, and a beam support can be constructed for either end. The central beam, measuring 3m (10ft) can then be inserted to join the two end sections together (*see diagram on page 54*).

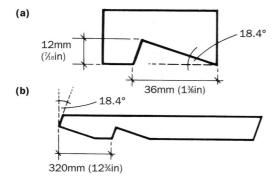

(a)

12mm
(⁷⁄₁₆in)

18.4°

36mm (1⅜in)

(b)

18.4°

320mm (12¾in)

Rafters – the bird's mouth.

In order to construct the roof framework, make up four end rafters from the 2.7m (9ft) lengths of timber, cutting 19-degree angles at each end. Measure 30cm (12in) from one end and cut a bird's mouth into the underside of the timber, which will allow the rafter to rest on the supporting wall at the correct angle.

To complete the roof framework, another eight rafters of 3m (10ft) in length need to be cut and each one should have 19-degree angles at each end, and bird's mouths cut into them at the same measurements as the end rafters. These should then be attached within the roof framework at spaces of 60cm (24in).

Roofing
The plywood sheeting should be cut so that it can be nailed securely to the rafters.

Cladding
When nailing cladding to the framework, it is usually best to start at the bottom and work upwards. The type of cladding used will depend on the preferred finish, as does the method of joining the boards together. For example, a tongue-and-groove, or

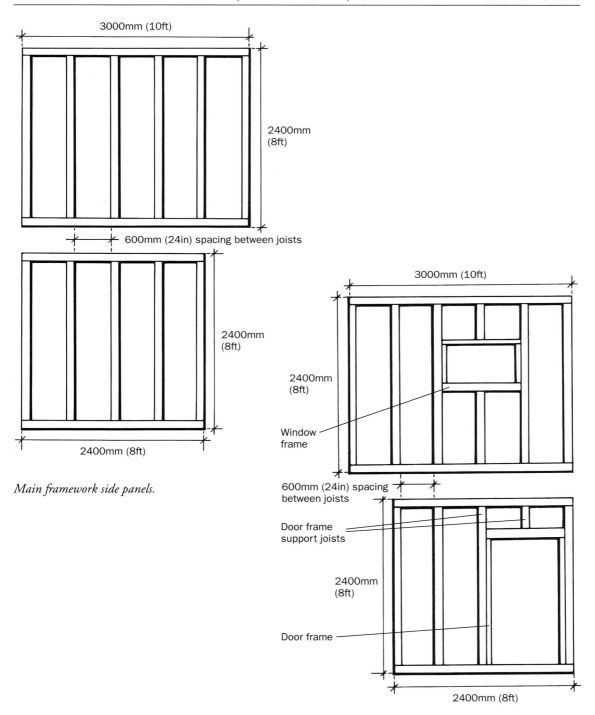

3000mm (10ft)

2400mm (8ft)

600mm (24in) spacing between joists

2400mm (8ft)

2400mm (8ft)

2400mm (8ft)

Main framework side panels.

3000mm (10ft)

2400mm (8ft)

Window frame

600mm (24in) spacing between joists

Door frame support joists

2400mm (8ft)

Door frame

2400mm (8ft)

Main framework door and window panels.

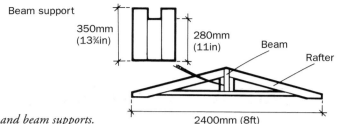

Beam support
350mm (13¾in)
280mm (11in)
Beam
Rafter
2400mm (8ft)

End rafters and beam supports.

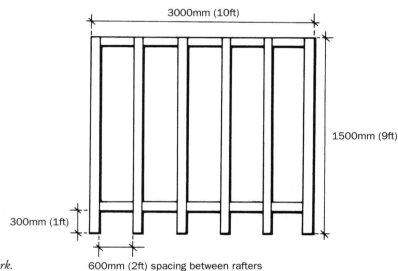

3000mm (10ft)
1500mm (9ft)
300mm (1ft)

A roof framework.

600mm (2ft) spacing between rafters

shiplap cutting will slot into each other, whereas waney-edged or feather-edged cladding overlaps each panel.

Roofing Material

Attach the roofing felt using the same methods as for fastening roofing felt to a pre-assembly type building (*see* pages 42 and 44).

Fascia and Eaves Boards

Cut the fascia boards at 90-degree angles to match the rafters and nail them in position then place and nail the eaves boards in the correct position.

Doors

First, fit any handles and locks onto the door. Hold the door against the frame and mark the door so that it can be planed to size. Mark the position on the frame where the locking mechanism is going to be so that when the door is hung, the door mechanism will be in line with any frame furniture. The door can then be hung using the same methods as for hanging a door on a pre-assembly type building (*see* pages 45–6).

Windows

Put the window into position and nail into the frame. If it needs to be glazed, measure the opening in the frame, deduct 3mm (⅛in) from all sides to get the right measurement and then cut the glass to size. If possible, it is best to have this done by a professional, as glass is quite difficult to cut and can be dangerous if you are unsure how to do it. Fit the glass into the frame, tap in small wire nails to hold the glass in position, and then apply putty or glazing beads.

CHAPTER 4

Decking, Steps, Walkways and Bridges

DECKING

Decking first gained popularity in Scandinavia and the USA. Now it is a common sight in British gardens and features in many landscape designs. A deck can be built on almost any terrain without levelling or filling. It can be raised slightly above ground, or several metres above ground level. In either case, it can transform land into living space that would not otherwise have been used either because it was considered completely unsuitable, or judged to be too difficult or expensive to convert into useable terrain.

A deck is a very flexible type of hard surface because it can easily be built around trees and other obstacles. It can provide a solution to the problem of landscape features that are difficult or expensive to remove, such as large rocks or old footings. It can be

installed easily over the features concerned, whereas a traditional deck would require the ground to be level and any obstacles to be removed.

Decking does not have to be set all at one level. It can be multi-tiered, which makes it ideal for use in gardens that are on a slope.

It can also be set up as walkways to make places such as meadows or nature conservation areas accessible. Where it is difficult to transport materials, a tile-type decking system can be used as long as the ground is fairly level and firm. The decking tiles are reasonably light to transport and easy to lay, which makes them ideal for this type of situation.

Decking can also be used to enlarge living space – a deck acts as an ideal outdoor living area, which can either be attached to the house, or set apart as a raised viewing or general recreational area.

A raised deck on a sloping site.

DESIGNING A DECKED AREA

Decking is predominately used to create an outside living area that can be used for dining or as a general recreational area where people can sit and talk, or just admire the view. Therefore it is essential that the deck be constructed in the right position, which may be directly outside the house, outside a summerhouse, or even in a central or secluded part of the garden. You need to establish what purpose the deck is to be used for and then walk around the garden so that you can decide where it should be built. When making this decision, the following should be considered:

- If the deck is to be used mainly in the evenings, a shaded spot can be chosen as the sun will not play an important factor in your plans. However, if the deck is to be used mainly in the daytime, a sunny or partially shaded position would be the best choice.
- If the area to be used is open to the prevailing winds, consider whether a windbreak could be erected. If so, this needs to be included in the design.
- If privacy is a major factor, a ground-level deck would be preferable to a raised one, otherwise you will be on full view and it could also cause disputes as it may affect the privacy of your neighbours.
- The ultimate size of the deck should always be considered. In order to assess this, it is best to mark out the size and shape of the proposed deck with sand. Stand back to view the area then walk inside. If the initial design does not fulfil your requirements, the sand marked area should be erased, marked again and re-assessed.

Lighting

This is a major consideration when designing your deck. It needs to be decided during the planning process and not as an afterthought because it is a lot easier to incorporate during construction rather than at a later stage. Lighting is essential if the deck is to be used at night. When deciding where the lights are to be situated, and the type of lighting to be used, the following points should be taken into consideration:

- The deck area should not be over-lit, as lower light levels will enhance the beauty of the deck, and will help to create a more relaxed atmosphere.
- Obstacles, such as changes in levels and steps that may need to be lit up.
- Lights should not be situated where they will shine into neighbouring houses and gardens; or where an unpleasant glare is caused, especially where the deck is situated near to public highways, as it may cause a hazard to motorists.
- The lights should be placed so that they are not obtrusive but they should be easy to reach so that the changing of bulbs and the cleaning of lenses is a simple operation.

Colour
Coloured lenses are available for most types of lights and by changing the colours you can enhance the visual effect and also create a more relaxing atmosphere.

Cables

Cables or wiring should be concealed within the framework using conduits, or buried underground to a depth of at least 46cm (18in).

General Safety Considerations

When planning the deck area it may be necessary to install waterproof electric sockets. When considering any type of electrical wiring, advice should be sought from a professional electrician.

Because of the obvious fire risks, a deck is not a suitable place for building a permanent barbecue area or even as a place to use a portable barbecue. If a barbecue area is required, the base for this should be constructed of a non-flammable material, such as paving slabs or concrete. It should be positioned far enough away from the decked area so as not to be a fire risk but near enough to allow cooked food to be served and eaten there.

Decking is renowned for having a slippery surface and therefore grooved boards should always be used. Moreover, when installing decked walkways, especially in shaded areas where the boards can become even more slippery, it is a good idea to nail galvanized chicken wire over the surface to provide extra grip.

When choosing the timber for decking, it is best to select high-quality planed wood and decking boards to avoid rough patches and sections that contain splinters. If this problem does occur, the timber should be sanded down.

Where steps are to be built, or there are raised deck areas, it is essential that hand and safety rails are included within your design.

The frames and supports are especially important when constructing raised decking areas. If timber of insufficient size is used there is a chance of the decking collapsing or warping. It is also essential that the spacing between timbers is adequate (*see* page 58).

In areas where there is a chance of rodent damage, special measures should be taken as they can damage wiring, or burrow under any footings and weaken them. Therefore, on low-level decks the underneath should be blocked off using wooden boarding or bricks in order to prevent this.

TYPES OF DECKING

There are two basic types of decking: the first incorporates prefabricated decking tiles; the second is of a traditional construction and consists of decking boards attached to wooden joists that can either be laid directly onto the ground or supported above it.

Decking Tiles

Decking tiles can be purchased ready-made, or you can construct your own.

They are quick and simple to lay and easily transported to areas where access is difficult.

Making a Decking Tile

Decking tiles can be made to any size but the following instructions are based on building tiles 90cm (3ft) square because they are easy to move and manoeuvre, fairly light, and a large area can be laid out quite quickly. The exact size of the tile should be worked out before it is made and then the length and width of the timber can be calculated accordingly.

Materials

Pressurized timber should be used for the decking boards. The size of board can vary depending on the finish required. Each board should be cut to the desired length and then nailed onto a framework

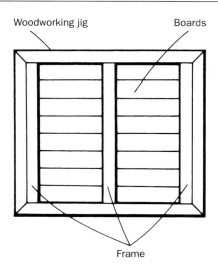

Construction of a decking tile.

made up of 5cm (2in) square, rough-cut timber. The frame should be constructed of three boards cut to 90cm (3ft) lengths with one at each end, and one in the middle. The pre-cut boards should then be nailed onto the framework, leaving a gap of 4mm (³⁄₁₆in). To make this process easier and quicker, and also to ensure that each tile is of equal dimensions, it is necessary to construct a woodworking jig, which is made up of scrap pieces of timber with an inside dimension slightly larger than 90cm (3ft) square, so that the framework fits neatly inside it but can be removed easily once the tile has been constructed. Also, it is necessary to mark where the edge of each board is going to be on the two sides of the jig where the decking boards are to be attached. This will ensure that all the boards are level and also that the spacing of the decking boards is exactly the same, so when they are laid each tile can be perfectly aligned.

Once the tile has been constructed, cut eight plywood spacers 4mm (³⁄₁₆in) thick and approximately 10cm (4in) in length and attach them to each corner of the frame. This will ensure that the tiles are evenly spaced when laid.

Laying the Tiles

The tiles need to be laid onto a firm and level surface. If one is not available, it can be constructed by either using concrete or hardcore. Where this is not possible, one can be made using a framework of pressure-treated beams measuring 10cm (4in) square, laid out with appropriate spacing between the beams to accommodate the tiles. The tiles can then be nailed to the beams.

However, if they are to be laid directly onto a firm level base, they can be held in place by erecting a timber framework around the tiles, which is sunk half-way into the ground and concreted in, ensuring that the top of the frame is flush with the top of the tiles. When laying the tiles onto a hard surface, it is recommended that a 2.5cm (1in) layer of sharp sand is spread across the surface and a level shovel of cement mixed in with each square metre of sand. The reason for doing this to ensure that the tiles bed in – the cement will eventually set which will help hold the tiles in position. When undertaking this operation, it is essential that you ensure that each row is in line and that the tiles are level: the tiles should be gently tapped with a rubber mallet to bed them into the sand and a spirit level should be used to ensure that they are level.

TRADITIONAL DECKING TERMINOLOGY

When discussing traditional decking construction, various terms are used and in order to understand how a deck is constructed, this terminology needs to be explained:

Footings

Concrete is the traditional material used for the footings that support the deck. The footings are usually 30cm (12in) square, 15cm (6in) deep and are built on firm ground. Alternatively, concrete blocks can be used. Footings are used to support the deck above the ground, with the minimum recommended size being 10cm (4in) square.

Posts

Posts are used to support the deck above ground level and can be concreted either directly into the ground, or attached to concrete blocks using metal fittings. The size of the posts is dependent on the weight of the deck and its anticipated usage.

Beams

The beams are attached to the tops of the posts, and the size of the beam determines the spacing and size of the posts with the larger beams requiring wider posts and greater spacing than smaller beams.

Joists

These are supported by the beams and create the framework to which the decking boards are attached. The joists should be fixed at 40cm (16in) intervals. This prevents the boards from being too flexible, which would create bouncing when the deck is used. The joist construction is dependent upon the pattern and design of the deck. Ledger boards are another type of joist that are fixed to a building such as the wall of a house.

Noggins

Noggins are used between the joists to make the framework more rigid.

Deck Boards

The width of a deck board should not be more than 15cm (6in). Using decking boards greater than this size makes warping of the wood more likely, which would in turn create an uneven surface.

Gaps

When the boards are laid, a gap is left between them that allows for swelling when wet without warping.

Even gaps between the decking boards.

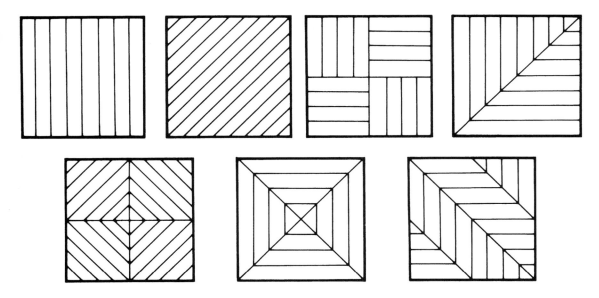

Decking patterns. Patterns can vary to suit individual designs.

Decking Patterns

The decking boards are the most visible part of the construction; therefore it is important that you choose the most suitable decking pattern. There are basically seven types of patterns available and these are illustrated above. It is worth noting that with the more complicated and intricate patterns, additional supports may be necessary.

DECK CONSTRUCTION

Ground-Level Decks

The following instructions are for the construction of a basic deck of 2.4m (8ft) square, built at ground level. They can be adapted to build any size of ground-level deck area by increasing or decreasing the amount of timber required. That amount can easily be calculated by using the recommended spacing and size of timber.

The Base

Mark out a base measuring 2.4m (8ft) square using a builder's square, pegs and lines. Once this has been done, using spray paint, mark along the lines and then remove them. The joists that will support the

deck need to be spaced at 60cm (24in) intervals. Measure in from the sides and mark out where the footings are going to be. The joists need to be 10cm (4in) square, so dig out a trench 15cm (6in) wide and 20cm (8in) deep to accommodate the footings.

Depending on the type of ground, and the overall size and purpose of the deck, either a concrete or concrete block base can be constructed. The latter is

An example of a ground-level deck.

an easier and cheaper option, with the blocks being placed on a firm bed of grit sand at 60cm (24in) spacings. However, this method should only be used for small areas and on ground that is fairly stable.

Whichever base is used, the levels must be checked both in each row and across the rows. It is also important that a weed-suppressant fabric is laid over any bare earth that is going to be under the deck because moisture may seep through and, together with some light, will encourage weed growth. The weeds will grow through the boards and be very difficult to control.

Joists

If using concrete footings, allow forty-eight hours before laying the joists onto them. Lay them across the centre of the footings and ensure that the ends of the joists are in line with each other. They should then be checked to ensure that they are level and secured in place. This can be done by attaching 5cm (2in) angle brackets at the end of the joists on each side with 5cm (2in) screws, so that there are four brackets on each joist. Mark the position of the brackets onto the footings and drill the holes into the footings to a depth of 5cm (2in), insert raw plugs, and secure in place.

Decking Boards

For laying a straight-board effect, start at one end and lay the first board across the joists, ensuring that the board is level with the end of the joists. Drill through the board and about 5cm (2in) into the joist; two holes should be drilled per joist. Use a countersunk bit on the planks for a flush finish and then screw in place. Start to lay the remaining boards, screwing each one in place and leaving a gap of 4mm (⁵⁄₁₆in) using spacers between each plank and ensure that the final board is flush with the joists.

If you require a diagonal pattern, cut one end of all the boards at a 45-degree angle, ensuring that the angle runs in the right direction. The angled board should be attached flush with the end joist at one end and each of the boards should be approximately 25cm (10in) longer than what is required. After the boards have been attached, using a circular or hand saw, cut the excess off level with the second outer joist, which ensures a well fitting, neat finish.

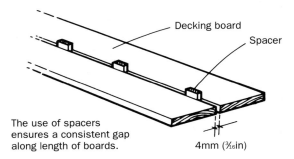

The use of spacers ensures a consistent gap along length of boards.

4mm (⁵⁄₁₆in)

Correct spacing of decking boards.

Diagonal boards should be laid using a square so that the correct angle is achieved, starting at one end laying the part that has been cut at a 45-degree angle flush with the joists, leaving a 4mm (⁵⁄₁₆in) gap between the boards using spacers.

If laying decking against a wall, a 4cm (⁵⁄₁₆in) gap still needs to be maintained between the wall and board, whatever pattern is being used.

Fascia Boards

The fascia boards give a neat finish to the deck, and should be nailed into the joists using two nails per joist. Cut two of the boards so that they will be flush with the end joists, and attach them to either end of the deck. Once this has been done, cut the other two boards so that they overlap the first two boards to give a level finish, and then nail them into position.

Split-Level Decks

Decking that is laid at different levels is one way of adding height and interest to a seemingly level garden.

One way of doing this is to lay one deck directly onto a ground-level deck to give a tiered effect. In order to do this, first make up a frame that is the same level as the deck that it is going to be laid on, which should be of sufficient length to accommodate the second-tier joists. Once this has been done, fill the frame with compacted hardcore, and then lay the footings in the same way as the ground-level deck, bearing in mind that some of the second-tier joists need to be screwed onto the first deck. The joists for the top deck must run at right angles to those used on the first tier, the reason for this being that it gives the decking extra strength, and also alters the direction of the deck boards, which enhances the visual impact of the deck and accentuates the height difference at each level. When the joists are in position then the second tier can be constructed using the same method as for the first tier.

Raised-Level Decks

A decking area can be raised by using posts to support the joists. This is especially useful on uneven or sloping sites where it would be either impossible or very difficult to build a conventional ground-level patio. Raising the deck even a short distance off the ground allows good air circulation, which helps the deck to dry more quickly when wet and thus prolong its life.

The first step in the process is to mark out the area and locate where the supporting posts are to be positioned. The posts should be positioned 90cm–1.2m (3–4ft) and 1.2m (4ft) apart, depending on the height and size of the decking – the higher and larger the deck, the nearer the posts need to be positioned. If the deck is to be next to a house wall, the posts adjacent to that wall need to be positioned 14cm (5½in) away from it. This will allow the beams that support the joists to be flush with the wall, facilitating installation of the decking right up to it. By using this method it is possible to avoid having to fix the deck to the house wall. The posts themselves need to be 10cm (4in) square and made of pressure-treated timber. It is essential when they are fixed that the footings are done correctly (*see* below) and that the posts are plumb as this maximizes their strength, which is important because they support the deck beams and the weight of the deck is transferred to the footings.

There are two ways in which the posts can be fixed into the ground. As with all posts, they can be concreted directly into the ground with 46cm (18in) of the post below ground level. Once the concrete surrounding the posts has set they can be cut to the desired height. This is achieved by cutting the first post to the required level. Working from this post and using a straight piece of wood and spirit level, the remaining posts can be cut so that they are all level with each other. This method is ideal for use on

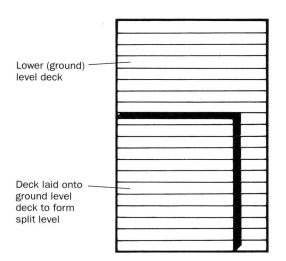

Split-level decking.

uneven ground and is a quick and easy way to install posts. However, it has one main disadvantage: because the posts are below ground they can rot and it is not easy to replace them.

Metal post anchors set onto concrete plinths can also be used. In order to do this, work out how many holes are required and then make up wooden frames or boxes measuring 25cm (10in) square and 17.5cm (7in) in height for each of the holes. Dig a hole to a depth of 30–46cm (12–18in), depending on how firm the ground is. Once this has been done, working from the lowest point, fill the first hole with concrete to ground level, and then put the wooden frame on top of the concrete base and check that it is level. This can then be filled with concrete to the top and levelled off. Then one of two methods can be adopted: either you can set a 'J'-bolt into the concrete whilst it is wet; or you can drill into the concrete once it has set, so that the metal anchors can be secured.

Whichever method is used, it is essential that the bolts, or anchors, are in the centre of the footing and that they are perfectly straight. On relatively even ground, after the first footing has been built, you should use a straight piece of wood and spirit level to ensure that the top of the next footing is level with the first. This method and construction procedure should be used for each footing in turn.

In the figure, labels read: "Lower (ground) level deck" and "Deck laid onto ground level deck to form split level".

Concrete plinths.

The deck beams.

Countersinking the bolts.

Alternatively, if the deck is to be constructed on an uneven or sloping site, use the same method as when levelling posts set in concrete (*see* page 61). Once the metal anchor is fixed in position, cut each of the posts to the desired height, place the post into the anchor and secure into position with galvanized nails. The main advantage of this method is that because the posts are not below ground level they will not rot as quickly. In addition, they are easier to replace if they do rot as the footings do not need to be dug out – the old rotten post can be simply removed from the anchor, and a new post fitted.

If either of these methods are used on ground that is prone to waterlogging, it is a good idea to put a 7.5cm (3in) layer of gravel in the footing hole before putting in the concrete as this will provide drainage underneath the footing.

As with any deck, weed-suppressant fabric should be spread over the bare earth underneath and pegged in position. With a raised deck, the underneath will usually be visible and therefore the fabric should be covered with pea-gravel to give a neat finish. Once this has been done, the deck beams can be installed, which will consist of two planed 15×5cm (6×2in) timber boards. These should be fixed either side of the supporting posts, with the top edge of the boards being level with the top of the posts.

Attach the beams to the supporting posts with approximately 14cm (5½in) overhang at each end, using 17.5cm (7in) decking bolts. The beams should first be nailed in position. Once this has been done, drill straight through both boards and the post; two bolts should be used for each post. At either side of the post it may be necessary to countersink the holes if the bolts are not long enough to fit to the beams.

The next step involves screwing 7.5cm (3in) square joists to the beams for added strength. The best way of doing this is to screw in at an angle from the sides of the joists into the beam. The joists need to be fitted approximately 46cm (18in) apart, which is slightly closer together than the spacings used for a ground-floor deck. The reason for this is that once the deck is raised off the ground, it is important that the structure is made even stronger.

Once all the joists have been put in place, the decking boards can be nailed into position. Finally, fascia boards can be nailed along the edges of the framework to ensure a neat and attractive finish.

STEPS

The purpose of steps is to allow access to and from the deck to the garden or from one level to another. They also help determine the flow of pedestrian

Evenly spaced joists attached to the beams.

traffic across the deck. When designing or considering steps, safety and ease of use must be the major consideration rather than overall appearance.

When deciding where the steps should be built, remember not to site them tight against a fence or other structure, as the steps will expand and cause damage. Attention should also be paid to how the deck will fit in with the rest of the garden and this may have some bearing on where the steps are situated.

Once the position has been decided, measure the vertical drop (the vertical distance from the top of the deck to where the stairs will end). The horizontal span should also be measured from the same two points. If a landing is to be incorporated into your stairway design, two horizontal measurements should be considered – the distance from the top of the deck to the edge of the landing platform, then from the landing to where the steps will finish on the ground. As a guideline, the horizontal span of the staircase should be 40–60 percent greater than the total vertical drop. However, if a landing is to be incorporated then the size of the landing should not be included. If the horizontal span is not 40–60 percent greater than the vertical drop, the point where the stairs finish should be moved back until an acceptable calculation is arrived at. Once these measurements have been taken, the next task is to work out the size of the steps required so that the number of steps to be built can be calculated.

The risers, which are the vertical depths, should measure 10–20cm (4–8in). The horizontal length of the steps, known as the run, must measure at least 23cm (9in). It is considered that the safest, most comfortable to use, and aesthetically pleasing steps should have a combined rise and run measurement of approximately 46–50cm (18–20in). The stair width is also important, and should measure a minimum of 90cm (3ft) if space allows, as this will enable two people to walk up the stairs together, or pass safely when walking in opposite directions.

There are basically three types of steps – the simplest of these and the easiest type to construct is the box step. This has a relatively strong construction but is more suitable in situations where smaller numbers of steps are required – the maximum number is usually three. The depth for the risers on this type of step is usually either 10cm (4in) or 15cm (6in) because this is a standard timber size and it eliminates the need for the timbers to be cut to fit.

The second type of step is where the step treads are joined between two pieces of wood. These are called stringers and usually measure 25×5cm (10×2in), or 30cm (12in). This method is ideal where large numbers of steps are required.

The stacked-deck step is very similar in construction to the split-level deck and is predominately used in larger gardens because steps of this type require more space than traditional ones.

Whatever types of steps are chosen, it is essential that a concrete footing is put in place at the base of the stairway provide support. The depth of the footing is dependent on the size of the stairway and also the type of ground. However, as a rule, the footings may vary in depth from 20–30cm (8–12in).

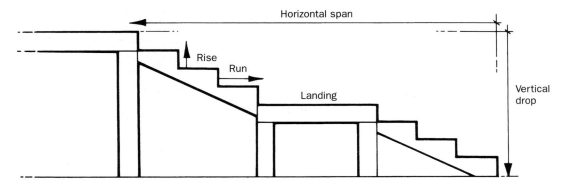

A simple step plan incorporating a landing and showing areas of measurement for calculation purposes.

Constructing Steps

Steps can be bought either as a complete unit or even in kit form; however it is also possible to build your own.

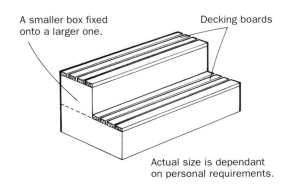

A smaller box fixed onto a larger one.

Decking boards

Actual size is dependant on personal requirements.

Box step construction.

Box Steps

A base frame should be constructed using screws. The frame should be the same width as the tread and its length equal to the combined length of all the stair treads. For example, if three steps are to be constructed, and each of the steps has a tread of 46cm (18in), and is 90cm (3ft) wide, then the base section needs to be 1.4m (4ft 6in) long and 90cm (3ft) wide. Another two sections should be made up, both 90cm (3ft) wide, with one of them being 90cm (3ft) in length, and final frame measuring 46cm (18in). The frames should then be placed on top of each other,

The frames can be joined together by using off-cuts attached to the inside of the frames at the sides and at the back. Once this has been made up, measure and cut the treads from decking boards, and screw into position, all except for the bottom step. The decking boards can be cut either so that they are flush with the edges, or so there is an overhang on both the front and sides, which gives a more finished effect. If an overhang is used, it is recommended that this should be no more than 12mm (1in).

When the steps are finished, lift them into position, and secure to the deck by driving deck screws through the back of the deck and into the stairway frame. Once this has been done, attach the base frame of the steps to the concrete footing using brackets and bolts attached to the inside of the frame. Once it is secure, the decking boards can be fixed to the bottom step.

Stringers

There are two types of stringers that can be used. The first is by attaching angle brackets to the stringers and then the tread boards can be screwed between them.

Alternatively, cut-out stringers can be used, which can either be purchased ready-made or you can cut your own. If you decide upon the latter, the easiest way to do this is to buy a stringer with either two or three cut-outs for the steps, and then use this to create as many steps as required. If cut-out stringers

are chosen then the stairs can also be boxed in if required. In order to attach the steps to the stringers, angle brackets should again be used. If the stairway is to have more than three steps or if the steps are to be more than 90cm (3ft) then a central cut-out stringer should be used. To join the steps to the deck, use angle-brackets, and also drive screws through the back of the deck into the stringers. The best method to attach the stringers to the footings is to secure

Stringer steps with yellow edging strips for the visually impaired.

Stringer steps leading up to the landing, which is secured to the building and held up at the front edges with support posts.

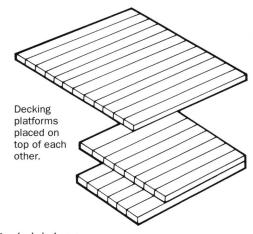

Decking platforms placed on top of each other.

Stacked-deck steps.

wooden cleats with bolts to the footings, and then place the steps in position and screw the stringers to the cleats.

Landings can also be included in your stairway design where the steep incline of the stairway is a major concern, or where a landing can form a platform that facilitates a change in the direction of a stairway. Landings can also be used to enable the creation of a platform from which two separate sets of steps can be created leading in different directions. The landing should be the same size as the width of the steps, for example if the stair width is 90cm (3ft) then the landing should be 90cm (3ft) square. The landing itself is constructed as a raised deck, and is held in position with support posts, which should be reinforced with cross-braces between them.

Stacked-Deck Steps

Stacked-deck steps are built using the same methods as the split-level deck – basically placing decking platforms on top of each other to create a tiered effect (*see* diagram below). They are secured on top of each other using decking screws, driven at angles through the sides of the deck into the lower section.

RAMPS

Ramps are traditionally associated with disabled access but they may also need to be installed where wheelbarrow or even pram access is required. However, a ramp is not a substitute for steps, and should be used only where an alternative access point is required, and the deck is large enough to allow it. However, if public access is allowed, you are obliged by law to supply access for the disabled, and therefore a ramp is a necessity.

The construction process used for a ramp is very similar to the one used in building a deck. Basically, the main difference is that instead of laying the joists at the same level on a concrete footing, the following method should be adopted.

Starting at the lowest point, where the deck is going to finish, lay the footing so that when the joist is fixed to it, the decking boards are at ground level. A line should then be attached from this joist to where the ramp is to be attached to the main deck, which will give you the fall of the ramp. The supporting

A ramp with a gentle gradient leading up to a door for disabled access. Handrails have been fitted because of the drop at either side.

posts and joists can then be installed using the line as a guide, the decking boards attached and the ramp completed.

HANDRAILS

The main reason for installing handrails is for safety. When stairways are installed that are three or more steps high then handrails are essential. Similarly, handrails must be fitted to ramps that are more than 3m (10ft) long, and have a gradient of 1:16, or steeper. Also, if a deck is to be built 50cm (20in) or higher, for safety reasons it is a legal requirement that handrails are installed. However, as well as being a safety requirement, handrails can also be aesthetically pleasing, and they can be used to highlight an area of decking, or add height to it, in order to improve its visual appearance.

When designing and constructing handrails, it is not only important that they are secure and that they can withstand the pressure of people leaning against them, but also that they should blend in with the deck and surroundings, enhancing their visual appearance. Also, in windy situations, or where the decking is overlooked, it may be necessary to increase

the height of the handrails and install solid panels. However, if it is desirable or necessary to have transparent panels, Perspex or toughened glass can be installed within the handrail frame, as this provides protection from the wind and ensures safety standards are maintained. On raised deck areas where young children have free access, solid panels should certainly be considered and if open railings are chosen then using wire mesh fitted between the rails may be a viable option. As for the height of handrails, it is recommended that they should be at least 1m (3ft 4in), and that this height should be increased to 1.4m (4ft 8in) in particularly hazardous situations.

Constructing Your Own Handrails

For the main posts, use 10cm (4in) square timber. The length of the posts should be the post measurement that is to be above deck level, plus the width of the depth sides. If, for example, the post above deck level is 1m (3ft 4in), and the deck depth is 10cm (4in), then the posts need to be 1.1m (3ft 8in) in length.

The tops of the posts need to be cut square, and the bottoms cut at 45-degree angles, which gives a neat and less bulky finish when the posts are attached

Handrails can be decorative as well as a safety feature.

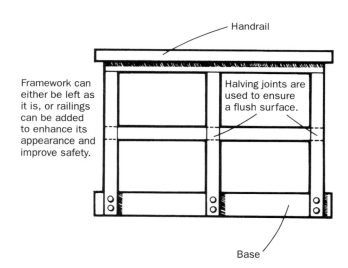

Handrail

Framework can either be left as it is, or railings can be added to enhance its appearance and improve safety.

Halving joints are used to ensure a flush surface.

Base

A framework plan for a handrail.

to the side of the decking. For the balusters, use 5cm (2in) square planed timber, which should be cut to the same length as the posts. The top of the baluster should be cut square and the bottom cut at a 45-degree angle. The number of balusters required depends upon the length of the handrails, the spacing between the balusters, which is usually about 10cm

(4in), and of course the width of the balusters themselves, which is 5cm (2in).

The posts then need to be attached with decking screws or bolts to the outside of the deck, with the angled edge being flush with the bottom of the deck. The posts should be spaced no further than 1.5m (5ft) apart. After all the posts have been secured,

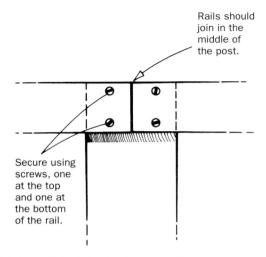

Rails should join in the middle of the post.

Secure using screws, one at the top and one at the bottom of the rail.

Joining rails by fixing in the centre of a post.

measure and cut 10×5cm (4×2in) × 5cm planed side-rails, and attach with screws so they are level with the tops of the posts. If more than one side-rail is required to finish a run then they should be fixed next to each other, so they join in the centre of the post.

This is the framework completed, so now the balusters can be attached using deck screws, with the angled edge level with the bottom of the deck. When fitting the balusters, use a block of wood 10cm (4in) wide as a spacer, to ensure that they are spaced at the same distance across the whole length of the rail. Finally, after all the balusters are in position, cut a piece of 15×5cm (6×2in), planed timber as a handrail. Fix this in position by screwing into the tops of the posts, and, as with the side-rails, if more than one rail is required, fit each rail flush with the next one in the centre of the posts.

WALKWAYS

Deck walkways can be used to access rough or wet areas where it would be impractical to lay any other type of hard surface. Many walkways are built in public places to facilitate access to areas such as water meadows. In this type of situation, the walkway should be at least 1.2m (4ft) wide, which is the minimum requirement for wheelchair users. However, if possible, the walkway should be 1.7m (5ft 8in) wide, which will enable either two wheelchairs to pass each other, or a pedestrian and a wheelchair user to pass each other safely. Moreover a walkway with a width of 1.7m (5ft 8in) allows a disabled person to walk with the aid of a helper and

A wooden walkway supported on posts.

other pedestrians to pass safely. However, in a domestic situation this may not be essential, although it is important that the width of the walkway suits the needs of the household.

The construction of a walkway is very similar to constructing a deck. The size of the joists should be a minimum of 15×5cm (6×2in), and if a long section of walkway is constructed then individual sections of approximately 3m (10ft) in length should be built.

The frame should be built to the required width and length using the same methods as adopted when constructing a decking frame. A central joist should be included to add strength to the frame and support the decking boards, which in turn will take the bounce effect out and make the walkway a lot smoother to walk on. Once the frame has been built, attach noggins (cross pieces) between the frame and central joists at 1m (3ft 4in) intervals, which will help make the frame rigid and reduce movement in the walkway. Once the frame has been constructed, it can be put into position; either supported on posts in the same way as a raised deck, or using timber sleepers or concrete blocks.

If concrete footings can be installed, this will help strengthen the framework. However, because this is a system that is used on unsettled ground, it can be difficult to install any type of footing. Therefore posts are usually hammered into the ground. The sleepers and concrete blocks are secured by tapping them into position. In particularly unstable areas, scalping or hardcore, to a depth of approximately 15cm (6in) should be laid and firmed before placing sleepers or concrete footings into position. Once the framework has been erected, the decking boards can be cut to size and nailed to the framework, allowing an even gap between the boards.

BRIDGES

A bridge can be a focal point that links various parts of the garden and it can be used either on its own, or in conjunction with walkways or decking.

In order to construct a simple bridge, the base should be built using the same procedures as those for a walkway with the length of the framework being 2m (6ft 8in) longer than the gap it is going to span, which allows 1m (3ft 4in) overhang at each side. The base can be straight, or if a curved effect is desired, specially shaped joists can be made up at timber yards or purchased from builder's merchants. For safety reasons, handrails should be fitted to the sides of the bridge. Depending on the length, weight, or position of the bridge, the handrails can be fitted before or after it has been installed. Footings should be constructed at either end of where the bridge is going to lie, and then it can be fixed into position.

Walkway boards, evenly spaced on straight runs and placed at angles where they curve, covered with galvanized netting for extra grip.

A bridge base placed in position.

JETTIES

Built at the edge of a pond or lake, a jetty is an ideal feature to relax on, fish or moor a boat. The jetty itself is built using the same methods as those employed to construct a ground-level deck. However, when building a jetty it is essential that no more than a quarter of the length overhangs the joist nearest to the bank, with 1m (3ft 4in) being the maximum overhang allowed. If the deck is going to be open plan to allow easy access to the water's edge and if there is no intention of installing handrails, consideration should be given to installing a low barrier, such as a 10cm (4in) square piece of timber attached by decking bolts to the edge or edges of the jetty that

ABOVE RIGHT: A decorative jetty deck at the edge of a pond without any safety features.

RIGHT: A wooden jetty on a lake with a raised front edge to prevent wheelchairs or buggies rolling into the water.

A decked area with pergola, planters and garden furniture.

face onto the water. Although this is not a physical barrier, it can act as a visual deterrent, and can be painted a different colour to the rest of the deck in order to highlight it. Also, in situations where the jetty is to be accessed by wheelchairs or pushchairs, the low barrier will help prevent them rolling into the water.

Timber railway sleepers set in a banking as steps.

OTHER FEATURES

Various features or additions, which can enhance the appearance of the deck include:

- Patio furniture
- Planted tubs or containers
- Water features, which can either be portable or purpose built

In addition to these features, any of the structures discussed in this book can be added.

RAILWAY SLEEPERS FOR PATHS AND STEPS

Railway sleepers have been used for many years in the construction of paths, steps and other landscape features. However, recent legislation which has proscribed the sale of creosote because of health worries, has also affected the sale and use of second-hand railway sleepers because of their creosote content. Notwithstanding this, the new legislation does allow second-hand sleepers to continue to be sold, as long as they are not to be used for children's play areas, toys, garden furniture, picnic tables, and inside buildings. However, it is

A timber railway sleeper seating area.

imperative that they are not used where there is a risk of frequent skin contact, or where they may come into contact with foodstuffs. It should be pointed out, however, that new untreated timbers as well as pressure or salt-treated timbers are readily available. All of these types of timber can be used in the construction of paths and steps, generally in conjunction with other materials, such as bark or gravel.

In addition to this, railway sleepers can be used as an alternative to decking, with the outer sleepers being drilled through at each end and held in position using metal spikes, which will then hold the inner sleepers in position.

WOODCHIP PATHS

Woodchip paths are widely used, especially in areas where a natural look is required. The woodchips are usually held in position with wooden edging boards. However, one of the main problems with this type of material is that it is a difficult surface for wheelchair users and it can become soft and unstable, especially in wet weather. To avoid this problem, lay a hardcore or concrete sub-surface, and then lay a 7.5–10cm (3–4in) layer of woodchip on top, which will help stabilize the path and form a firm surface.

A woodchip path, which blends with the surrounding plants to create a natural look.

CHAPTER 5

Fencing and Gateways

THE PURPOSE OF FENCING

The selection of the type of fencing to be used depends upon what purpose, or purposes, you wish the fence to serve. From prehistoric times, fences have served to keep trespassers out and livestock in, thus providing both privacy and protection. These factors still play a major part in modern-day living, and fencing may be required for all or some of the following reasons:

- A garden is considered by many people as an extension to the living area of the house, and the same degree of privacy may be required to enjoy the garden to its full extent.
- In exposed areas, or where strong winds can cause a problem, a fence can act as a windbreak. In these situations, it is best to choose a semi-permeable fence such as a picket, or netlon-type fence, which will allow the wind to filter through. A solid fence, rather than providing protection, is likely to cause damage through the wind hitting it, being forced over the top and forming an eddy. Also, there is more risk of the panel being broken by the wind.
- Where there is a risk of high noise levels, such as next to main roads or motorways, a solid fence can be erected in order to help reduce this. Shrubs or hedging planted behind the fence will reduce noise even further as they become established.
- By erecting either solid or permeable fencing in areas where there is a large amount of sunlight, especially in south-facing gardens, the garden may also be enjoyed in cooler weather, because it will give added protection.

- A fence can help with security, as it can act as a barrier in order to prevent entry into an area, or to prevent animals and children escaping from it.
- In some situations, a fence may be required to act as a screen, in order to hide unsightly areas, such as rubbish and compost bins, that may distract the eye from the beauty of the garden.
- Some landscape designs may include a variety of different zones, and fencing can be used to divide these areas.

TYPES OF FENCING

There are many different types of fences that can be used for purely practical reasons. However, a fence can also be chosen for decorative purposes, such as highlighting the boundary of land surrounding a property, which in turn can cause a visual illusion by extending the apparent size of a house

The types of fencing styles available are endless. First, however, you must decide whether to build the fence using ready-made fence panels or to construct your own from loose materials?

Ready-Made Panels

The main advantages of ready-made panels are:

- It is a simple process to work out the number of panels and posts required, as all panels are 1.8m (6ft) long.
- The panels are usually available in four heights – 90cm (3ft), 1.2m (4ft), 1.5m (5ft) and 1.8m (6ft), so that they suit a variety of purposes and will match in with most designs.

- They are fairly easy to erect, as the panels themselves are ready made and simply need to be fitted between the posts.
- Ready-made panels are widely available from DIY stores, builder's merchants, and timber merchants.
- The more widely used panels are relatively inexpensive.

However, ready-made panels tend not to be as strong as fences constructed from loose materials, as the panels are fixed between the posts and can be subject to wind damage. They can also shrink as they age, so that they do not fit as well as when they were first installed. Fences made from loose materials either overlap the posts or are fixed into the edges of the posts, which makes them a stronger option. Panel fences are not ideal for sloping ground as they will need to be stepped and also they are in set lengths of 1.8m (6ft) which means you cannot choose where the posts are going to be positioned. This in turn may mean that the bottom part of the fence panel needs to be buried in the slope, and as you work up the banking a series of longer posts are required.

Building Your Own Fence

Choosing to build a fence from scratch enables you to make your fencing to any design you wish,

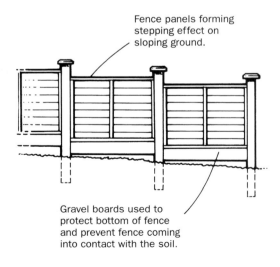

Fence panels forming stepping effect on sloping ground.

Gravel boards used to protect bottom of fence and prevent fence coming into contact with the soil.

Constructing a stepped panel.

customizing a basic design to meet your individual needs. The four main disadvantages are:

- They are usually more difficult to build.
- It is more complicated to work out the amounts of materials required.
- More materials are required, which makes it more expensive.
- The fencing materials are not always easily available and for some fencing applications, materials may need to be purchased from specialist timber merchants.

In addition to the above considerations, the purpose of the fence, and budget available, will be the main deciding factors.

FENCING PANELS

There are many different types of panels available, and some of the main ones are listed below:

Waney Lap

Probably the most commonly used panel fence, it comprises boards with irregular lower edges, which overlap to form a solid barrier, fixed a within a wooden frame, which is attached between the posts. Waney lap fence panels vary in strength and quality. The better quality panels usually have slightly thicker boards and additional vertical strengthening battens on the reverse side of the fencing.

Interwoven

An interwoven panel comprises thin pieces of wood, woven between a numbers of vertical battens in a basketweave pattern. These used to be the most popular panels because they were readily available, lightweight, and fairly inexpensive to buy. Their main disadvantages are that there can be gaps between the boards, which allow people to look through, and a lack of strength. They have now been largely superseded by the stronger waney lap fencing.

Trellis

Trellis panels can be used either on their own, or on top of a solid panel to give additional height, with their main purpose being to support plants. They are

A wattle hurdle fence panel.

Trellis fence panels.

available in either a square or a diamond pattern. Each panel is 1.8m (6ft) in length, and they are available in heights of 30cm (12in), 60cm (24in), 90cm (3ft), 1.2m (4ft), 1.5m (5ft), and 1.8m (6ft). Trellis panels are available in both lightweight and heavy-duty versions – the type chosen depends on how and where it is going to be used. The more flimsy panels are best for small heights and are usually intended as a fence top, or for fixing onto a wall, whereas the more heavy-duty panels are ideal for use in more exposed locations and can be used on their own in a fence, or attached to the sides of a pergola or similar structure.

Vertical Lap

This type of fence panel looks like a closeboard fence, and usually comprises 10cm (4in) straight-edged boards. They are stronger than either the waney lap or interwoven panel, but they are also more expensive.

Wattle Hurdle

This traditional 'Olde English' type of fencing is constructed using strips of flexible branches, generally willow. This type of panel has recently come back into fashion, and is now widely available in a range of sizes. The panels basically comprise branches woven around evenly spaced stout poles. This type of panel is fairly flexible and can also be used if a curved effect is required.

Bamboo and Willow Screen

This type of panel, comprising either bamboo or willow screen material set within a wooden frame, is a fairly recent innovation and ideal for adding a tropical or rustic theme to the garden.

Picket

A picket fence is available either in panels, or as a self-assembly kit. The pickets, or pales as they are sometimes known, are commonly available with flat, round or pointed tops. The panels can either be straight, concave or convex – the latter two can be used either on their own or together to form a gentle 'rollercoaster' effect.

SELF-BUILD FENCES

Picket

A self-assembly type picket fence can be used to suit individual designs. For example, the pales on picket panels are spaced at 3.8–5cm (1½–2in) intervals, but they can be spaced nearer or further apart to suit personal preferences when constructing a fence from scratch. Also, the pales can be lengthened or shortened to create either a curved or a zigzag effect.

Post and Wire

This type of fence is more practical than decorative, comprising wire mesh attached to wooden posts. The mesh can be galvanized or plastic-coated and is

A picket fence.

available in a range of different gauges. The smaller gauges are ideal for protecting crops from rodents such as rabbits, but it is important that at least 60cm (24in) is buried to prevent burrowing underneath it. The larger gauge is ideal for keeping livestock in or out, the plastic-coated mesh being best where a stronger fence is required.

Post and Rail

This is one of the simplest forms of timber fencing, comprising either two or three wooden rails attached to timber posts. The size of the posts and rails is dependent on their usage. This type of fence is used to highlight a boundary but is not suitable on its own for providing privacy or security. However, it can be used as a frame for attaching wire or willow-type fencing material. It is sometimes used in conjunction with a newly planted hedge, acting as a visible form of boundary until the hedge has established

Closeboard

This solid and durable fence has increased in popularity over recent years. It basically comprises boards of 10–15cm (4–6in) in width attached to arris rails

A post and rail fence.

The back of a closeboard fence.

Rustic fencing.

Willow fencing.

with the boards overlapping each other. This type of fence is ideal in situations where privacy is important and a strong fence is required.

Rustic

A rustic effect can be achieved by the use rustic poles or stakes to form a post and rail fence or a more elaborate construction by adding to the basic post and rail framework. Alternatively, a post and rail framework can be made using flat wooden rails and then half-round rustic posts can be attached.

Bamboo and Willow Rolls

Bamboo and willow fencing comes in rolls that can be bought in an assortment of lengths and the fencing itself is available in heights of up to 1.8m (6ft). The fencing material is also available in various grades, which is denoted by its expected life expectancy, but how long the material will last outdoors is also dependent on where the fence is constructed and how the fencing material is attached. It is imperative that a framework is constructed that the material can then be attached to, as the

An ornate willow living fence.

framework will give the fence strength. Without a suitable framework, the fence will become damaged at the first sign of wind because the material will move in the wind, which will weaken it and can cause it to split.

A Living Fence

This cross between a fence and a hedge is constructed by using freshly cut willow sticks and is best undertaken in either October or November so that the willow will root easily. As the material is very flexible, different patterns and shapes can be achieved including diamond and woven effects.

ERECTING FENCE POSTS

The way a fence post is fixed into the ground depends on several factors including the type of post that is to be used, the type of fencing and ground conditions. The main methods for erecting and fixing fence posts into the ground are as follows.

Concrete

Concreting posts into the ground is a method used for many types of fences including panel, closeboard, and post and rail. It is used in situations where the ground is not very firm and extra support for the posts is required. In order for the posts to be erected correctly the following procedure should be followed.

Dig a hole that allows approximately 15cm (6in) clearance around the post, and is 15cm (6in) deeper than the length of post to be buried. In order to speed up the process of digging the holes, a post hole borer or auger can hired, which comes in 10cm (4in), 15cm (6in) and 23cm (9in) diameters.

A layer of coarse rubble should be added to a depth of 15cm (6in), which provides a firm, but free-draining base.

The post should then be placed in the hole, ensuring that it is vertical, which can be checked using a post level. Once this has been confirmed, ram hardcore to approximately one-third of the depth of the hole, so that the post is held firmly.

Fill the remainder of the hole with a 5:1 part mix of ballast to concrete and slope the top of the concrete just below ground level, so that water does not gather on top of the post. To achieve a natural finish, place bare soil around the post once the concrete has set, which can then be grass seeded or turfed.

Set holding struts around the post to keep it in position. If fence panels are being used and they are going to be put up immediately, attach the struts to the edges of the posts that will not carry the panels.

Metal Post Spikes

This is a quick and easy method, which does not involve digging, and once the metal post spikes have been put in the ground, they are set in position.

However, it is imperative that the ground is firm and without too much rubble as this could prevent the post from going in straight.

As with all methods of fence erection, it is very important that the position of any underground services are located before work commences. However, it is especially important when using this method, as the spikes themselves are about 46cm (18in) long, and the result could be catastrophic if hammered through a mains electrical cable.

When hammering the post spikes into the ground, use either a metal post-driving tool or a block of wood placed inside the metal post socket, and hit with the hammer to prevent damaging it. As the spike is being hammered into the ground, stop occasionally and check with a spirit level to ensure it is going in straight. If not, straighten it up and repeat the procedure. When only the post socket is visible above the ground, remove the driving tool or block of wood and insert the post. The post is secured by

A post set in concrete.

Holding struts attached to a newly concreted post.

A metal fence spike, driving tool, fence clip and caps.

either clamping or screwing, depending on the type metal spike used.

If a long run of fencing is being erected, it is recommended that every third post is concreted in to add strength and stability. Also, it is a good policy to concrete in the end posts on both long and short runs as these are the posts that will weaken first as they are not boxed in like those in the middle.

Metal Bolt-Down Posts

This works on the same principal as the metal post spikes, in that the wooden post fits into the socket. However, with this type of fitting, it is possible to erect posts on top of walls and other hard surfaces without having to break them up

Driven Posts

Driving posts into the ground with a drivall or post hammer is the commonest method used when constructing wire fences connected to wooden posts and rustic fences among others. The fence posts used are generally referred to as stakes and can either be round, half-round or square, they are pressure treated and come in a variety of different lengths and diameters.

The easiest and safest method is to use a drivall when hammering in round stakes, as it is less likely to split or damage the top of the stake. Also, there is less chance of it slipping or bouncing off the stake as can happen when using a hammer. However, it is important to wear a hard hat because when taking the drivall off the stake, it can easily slip back and cause a head injury. When choosing a drivall, ensure that the diameter is wider than that of the post, because if it fits too tightly there is a possible. Whatever method is used, it is best to make a pilot hole first with a metal bar, which will help to ensure that it goes in straight. As with metal posts, it is essential that services are checked before commencing.

For larger posts, or in situations where many posts are to be hammered, a purpose-built machine can be hired.

Attaching Posts to a Wall

In some cases, it may be necessary to attach a post to a wall. In order to do this, 6mm (¼in) diameter self-expanding coach bolts should be used, the length of these being dependent on the width of the post. Two bolts should be used, one at the top and one at the

A drivall used for driving in fence posts.

Fencing fitted between brick pillars.

bottom, for posts under 1.5m (5ft) in height. For posts over this height, a third bolt should be used in the centre. In order to do this, you need to drill through the post, ensuring that the hole is slightly larger at the surface so that the bolt head is flush, which allows the panel to fit neatly against the post. Then hold the post against the wall, ensuring it is straight and level, and mark on the wall through the bolt hole. Remove the post, and drill the holes with a masonry bit. Put the post back into position and tighten the bolts, using wooden off-cuts between the wall and post if necessary to ensure the post is vertical – this can be checked with a spirit level.

Materials Used for Posts

The most popular posts used in the construction of wooden fencing are made from wood and concrete.

Fence panels can be fitted between brick or stone pillars, usually on top of a wall. The strength and durability of the brick or stone, matched with the natural beauty of the woods provides a visually attractive and secure barrier.

Concrete posts are used in situations where there may be a risk of vandalism, in particularly damp situations where wooden posts may rot, or where strength and durability, rather than appearance are the top priorities. Concrete can be supplied for post and rail fencing, though it tends to be mainly supplied and used for panel fences. This type of post

is ideal for situations where the panels may have to be removed occasionally to gain access to an area, because the panels are fitted into a groove on the side of the post, which allows you to slide the panels in and out easily. Concrete kick boards can be purchased to fit the posts if required.

Concrete posts and kick boards.

Gravel boards fitted at the bottom of a closeboard fence.

Gravel Boards

These can be made from either concrete or timber. When choosing a timber gravel board, it should be made from pressurized softwood, measure 15×3.8cm (6×1½in) and be the same length as the panels, which is 1.8m (6ft). Gravel boards are fitted at the bottom of the fence, which protects it from decay. This is particularly useful in damp situations, or where the panels come in contact with the soil, because it is a lot easier and cheaper to replace a gravel board than a fence panel.

ERECTING A PANEL FENCE

Locate where the first end post is going to be situated, excavate a hole and concrete it in, holding it in position with temporary props on three sides.

Run a string line from the end post to the end of the proposed fence run and pull tight. Measure the length of the panel, which is usually 1.8m (6ft) from the inner edge of post. Erect the second, either concreting in, or using a metal fence spike. If the post is to be concreted in, do not backfill with concrete, but hold in place by consolidating rubble around the base of the post and using temporary props.

The panel can now be put in position. Ensure it is the right way up, and if the panel has two different facing sides, ensure that the sides are facing the correct way. Place blocks underneath so it is not touching the ground, or in the case of gravel boards, ensure that blocks are used that allow enough space for the gravel board to be fitted.

ATTACHING FENCE PANELS

Once you are happy with the position of the panel it can be attached to the post using one of the following methods.

Nails

The cheapest and simplest way of attaching the panels to the posts is to nail through the outer

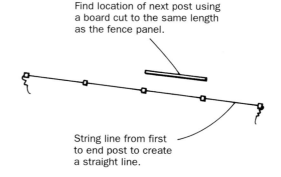

Find location of next post using a board cut to the same length as the fence panel.

String line from first to end post to create a straight line.

Marking out the posts for a panel fence.

frame of the panel into the post, using 7.5cm (3in) galvanized nails. The panel should be nailed at an angle to the top, middle, and bottom as this will give added strength, although with the 1.5m (5ft) and 1.8m (6ft) panels, additional nailing between the outer nails and middle nail is recommended. With some fence panels, especially where the outer frame is very thin, it is advisable to drill a pilot hole first before hammering in the nails to prevent it from splitting

Fence Panel Brackets

If the fence is going to be erected in an area where there are high winds, the use of fence panel brackets should be considered, as these provide a strong fixing, and the frame on the panels is likely to split in severe wind when nails are used.

There are two types of brackets. 'U'-shaped brackets have holes on the base plate, so that they can be nailed directly to the post. They also have holes in the side plates in order to secure the brackets to the panels.

The other type of fence panel bracket is the fence clip, which is nailed to the fence post. The bracket fixes around the frame of the panel, and is then secured by screwing or nailing it to the frame through a hole in the side of the clip. With this type of clip, you need to fix one underneath the other on either side of the panel. Clips are generally used at the top and bottom of panels up to 1.2m (4ft) in height. For panels higher than this, a third bracket or set of brackets should be used to attach the central edge of the panel.

Both types of bracket should be nailed to the fence post first, making sure that they are all in line. The panel should then be slid between the brackets and then nails or screws can be used to attach them to the panels. Screws are probably the best option, as this allows you to unscrew the panel as required and remove it easily either for access, maintenance or replacement.

Wooden Lats

This method is usually adopted in situations where access is required at least once a year, for example to fuel or maintain an oil tank. Wooden lats consist of two pieces of wood 19mm (¾in) square, nailed to the

'U'-shaped fence brackets holding a trellis fence panel in position.

inside edge of both posts where the panel is to be fixed and spaced so that the panel can be slid in and out fairly easily. A screw is usually put through one of the lats on either side, so that there is some security but it can easily be taken out when necessary.

Whatever the method chosen for fixing the panels in position, it is important to check that they are level both horizontally and vertically.

Once the panel has been fixed, if the post is to be concreted, this can be done now leaving two braces in position, one on each outside edge of the post. The procedure can then be repeated for each panel. This method ensures that each panel is level and fits

Vertical wooden lats holding a trellis fence panel in position so that it can slide in and out as required.

correctly. If the posts are put in before any panels, there is a risk in making a mistake with a measurement and it is very difficult to remedy the slightest error once the posts are in position, and if one post has to be moved then they all do.

If gravel boards are to be fitted, they can be fixed once the run of fence is completed (see page 84). In the case of posts that have been concreted in, wait until they have set and remove the blocks.

Finally, check that the top of each post is the same distance above the panel, if this is not the case, cut the same amount off each post so they are the same height as the shortest one. Apply preservative to the cut tops, and fix a fence cap on top using two nails, but first drill a small pilot hole, as these caps tend to split easily.

ERECTING A CLOSEBOARD FENCE

Closeboard fences are available as prefabricated panels, although the normal form of construction is to erect it on site, using separate components. The fence is basically constructed by attaching the arris rails to the fence posts, and then the boards are attached to the rails.

Rails and Posts

The rails can be either triangular or flat. The triangular rails usually measure 10×7.5×7.5cm (4×3×3in) and the flat ones 10×7.5cm (4×3in). Triangular rails offer greater resistance to the wind; therefore these are ideal for use in very open situations.

The posts themselves can be either solid or ready-mortised to take the arris rails. If the posts are solid, you need to cut the mortises yourself. In order to do this, you need to mark out where the rails are to be positioned, which is usually 30cm (12in), from the top and the bottom of the fence post.

If triangular rails are to be used, these are fixed in the sides of the posts. In order to do this, use a 2.5cm (1in) flat bit to drill out and then finish off with a chisel. The ends of the rails need to be chamfered in order to fit into the mortises. This is best done by using an axe, but it is important that not too much is taken off, otherwise it will not fit tightly, and a loose arris rail will make the whole fence unstable.

Flat rails are attached to the front of the posts, therefore a halving joint needs to be made, which can be cut out using a saw and chisel.

The alternative to these two methods when using solid posts, is to fit the arris rails to the posts using galvanized metal arris brackets, which is much

Chisel-ended rails.

Arris rails fitted to posts using a halving joint.

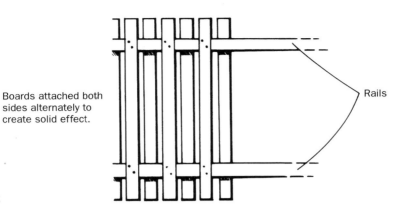

Boards attached both
sides alternately to
create solid effect.

Rails

Alternate fencing.

simpler, but probably not as visually attractive because the metal brackets can be seen.

If the fence is to be constructed using the mortised method, the posts and rails need to be erected at the same time, whereas if the flat rail method or arris rail brackets are used, all the posts in the fence run can be put up first.

With either of the methods, it is best to concrete the posts in because the construction of this type of fence is a lot heavier than panel fencing and a strong wind may loosen the posts more easily.

Boards

A traditional closeboard fence is constructed so that the boards overlap each other.

However, using the same framework method as employed closeboard fencing, it is possible to construct a fence that can give the same degree of privacy, but has the added advantage of looking the same from either side. If this method is chosen, flat arris rails should be used, and it is worth noting that access will be needed to either side of the fence in order to attach the boards.

Whatever the choice of arrangement of the boards, the construction technique is basically the same. The first thing that needs to be done, once the posts and arris rails have been put up, is to attach gravel boards measuring 15×2.5cm (6×1in) to the bottom of the fence.

If triangular arris rolls are used, support battens need to be nailed to the inner edge of the posts, and these should be sufficiently recessed to be flush with

the front of the post when the board is put in place. With the flat rail method, the gravel boards can be nailed to the front of the posts.

Once the gravel boards have been put in position, the boards can be put up. If feather-edged boards are used for closeboard fencing, the thicker edge of the board needs to be butted up against the post, or level with the edge of the post if flat arris rails are used.

Whatever type of board or board fencing is to be constructed, spacing is an important consideration and the following guidelines should be followed.

In the case of closeboard fencing, the thinner edge of the first board should overlap the thicker edge of the second board by 12mm (½in) and this procedure should be repeated to the end of the run. In order to ensure that this measure is consistent for the entire run of the fence, a spacing gauge should be made from a piece of wood.

If the boards are to be spaced, the actual spacing depends on the requirements of the fence. However, whatever spacing is decided upon, this should be uniform for the entire length of the fence, and again a spacer should be made and used to guarantee this.

As with the posts used for panel fencing, post caps can be fitted in order to protect them and improve their visual appearance. To complete the closeboard fence, a bevelled coping strip can be fitted on top of the boards for protection. The strip should be cut to size and placed on top of the boards then nails should be driven through the top of the coping at regular intervals so that the nails go into the top of the boards.

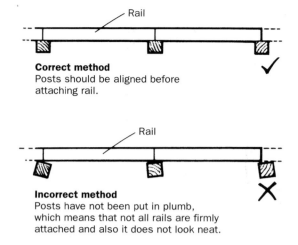

Correct method
Posts should be aligned before
attaching rail. ✓

Incorrect method
Posts have not been put in plumb,
which means that not all rails are firmly
attached and also it does not look neat. ✗

Post and rail fence construction.

Post and Rail, and Picket Fences

Post and rail fences are constructed in a similar way
to the flat arris rail framework for a closeboard fence,
although the rails are usually wider and they are
nailed directly onto the surface of the post.

Like a picket fence, a flat arris rail type framework can be used with the rails nailed directly to
the posts.

ERECTING A POST AND WIRE FENCE

This type of fence is erected using round, wooden
pressurized stakes, which are driven into the ground
at approximately 2.7m (9ft) intervals. The end posts
should have straining posts attached, and these
should be of the same material as the posts. In order
to fit them, a notch should be cut two-thirds up the
side of the post. A hole should be dug to the same
depth, approximately 46cm (18in) from the post,
and filled with compacted hardcore to about 15cm
(6in) from the surface. The brace then needs to be
put into position with one end cut to shape to latch
into the notch. The bottom of the brace should be
hammered into the hardcore to hold it in position.
The hole can then be topped up with additional
compacted hardcore or concrete. As well as being
used at the end of fence runs, straining posts should
be fitted in long runs, placed up to 1.5m (5ft) apart.

Once the posts have been put in position, the wire
fence material needs to be put up. This should be
tensioned, either by using a tensioning tool, or
straining wires can be used, which can be tensioned
using straining bolts. Attach the fence material using
metal fasteners, and attach the fence to the posts
using metal staples.

*Straining posts for a
post and wire fence.*

ERECTING A LIVING FENCE

A living fence is constructed by using un-rooted material, and this can either be bought in or you can take cuttings yourself. The cuttings are best taken from either willow or poplar trees after the leaves have fallen. The cuttings should be 1–2m (3ft 4in–7ft) in length and cut between two buds. Use a crowbar to make a hole and plant the cuttings directly into the ground to a depth of 30cm (12in) either straight or at angles, depending on the design required. A string line should be used to ensure a straight line.

GATES

Constructing a Gate

Designing and building your own gate is not too difficult a process. The main job is to construct the outer frame first, and this is basically the same whatever the interior design may be including vertical or horizontal boards, rails or any other infill material.

Making the Frame

The width and height of a gate will vary, but it is usually constructed from planed softwood. The frame is constructed first and consists of two 10×5cm (4×2in) side timbers, which should be cut at a slant or rounded to allow rainwater run off. The two horizontal timbers should measure 7.5×4cm (3×1½in). The timbers are joined together using tenon and mortise joints. When the timbers are cut to size, the length of the tenons on the horizontal timbers should be taken into consideration.

The simplest way to make this type of joint is to cut the tenons first, by putting the timber in a vice. The tenons need to be about 7.5cm×12mm (3×½in) wide. They should be marked out and the horizontal and vertical cuts made with a tenon saw. Once the tenons have been made, place them on a level, line them up with the vertical timbers and mark the position of the mortises. Place in the vice, and drill out a hole to the correct depth of 7.5cm (3in) using a 12mm (½in) auger bit. When this has been done, square off the sides using a wood chisel. When all the tenons and mortises have been cut, they should be

A home-made gate.

sanded and then joined together using wood glue, ensuring that the frame is square.

When the glue has set, the inner frame needs to be made. This consists of two pieces of 12mm (½in) square timber cut to the required length and attached using countersunk screws to the inner side of the top and bottom of the main frame. When the inner frame is in place, the chosen infill material can be attached.

The final stage of the gate construction is to fit a diagonal brace 10cm×19mm (4×¾in), between the top opening side corner and the bottom hinge side corner. Before fitting the brace, it needs to be cut so that it fits neatly. The way to do this is to cut the brace about 15cm (6in) too long, and then put it across where it is to be fitted. Mark the brace against the horizontal and vertical frame timbers, and saw off

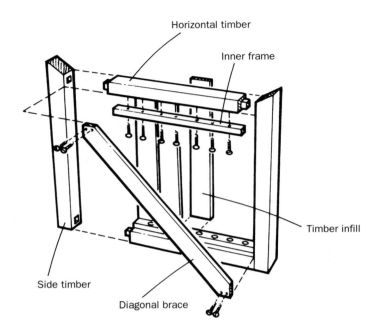

Constructing a frame for a gate.

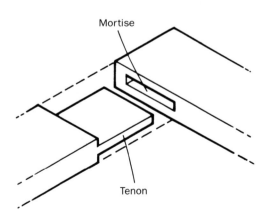

A tenon and mortise joint.

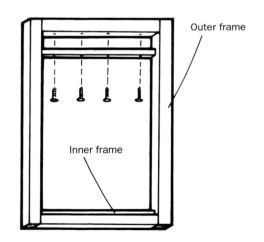

Constructing the inner frame.

the timbers as marked. This can then be attached to the inner frame on the opposite side to which the infill is secured.

Gateposts

Types of Posts

If timber gateposts are used, they should not be smaller than 10cm (4in) square. For a gate of more than 1.8m (6ft) high or 1m (3ft 4in) wide, this should be increased to 13cm (5in) square. If large and heavy gates are used then the post size should be increased to 15–17.5cm (6–7in) square.

The size of the gate determines the length of timber post required. For a gate of up to 1m (3ft 4in), you should allow for 46cm (18in) of the post to be buried in the ground, and for any gates above this height, at least 60cm (24in). If large and heavy gates are used, the posts should be long enough to allow for 1–1.2m (3ft 4in–4ft) of the post to be below ground level. Metal gateposts are also widely available with the fittings attached, which governs how deep the posts are to be buried.

Whichever of these types of posts are chosen, it is important that they are concreted in. A trench approximately 46cm (18in) deep should be dug between the posts, filled with a base of 15cm (6in) compacted hardcore and then topped with concrete, which will help to support the two posts .

Another possible method for both wooden and metal gates is to build brick pillars. These must be at least a brick and a half wide all the way round, and they should be built on a 46cm (18in) footing with approximately 46cm (18in) of the brickwork below ground level, so that the pillars are strong enough to support the gate.

Spacing the Posts and Concreting In

Once you have decided what type of post is to be used, the next stage is to determine where they are to be situated. One of the easiest ways to do this is to lay the gate in position on the ground, allowing an extra gap of 6mm (¼in) on either side of the gate for fittings. In the case of large or heavy gates it is usually easier to cut a piece of wood the same length as the gates with 12mm (1in) added on for the fittings, which can then be used as a measure.

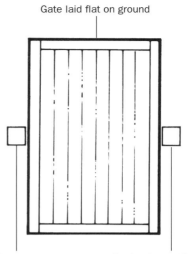

Gate laid flat on ground

Gate posts marked out allowing 6mm (¼in) either side for fittings.

Method for locating where the gateposts are to be erected.

The footings to accommodate the posts can be now dug to their required depth. The posts can be placed back in the hole, and the measurement checked before concreting in. Like the fence posts, the gateposts also need to be held in place until the concrete has set, which again is done with the aid of wooden struts.

Fitting the Gates

Before fixing the gate, check that it is to be hung at a height that allows sufficient clearance when fully open by putting it in that position, supported with bricks to the required height. Whatever final height is decided for the gate, there should also be a clearance gap of 6mm (¼in) either side of the gate. With single gates, the gate can be held in position by placing 6mm (¼in) wedges between the posts. Whilst doing this, the gate should be checked to ensure it is level before the position of the hinges is marked, and the gate fixed in position.

Other Fittings

As well as the hinges, a gate needs some type of shutting mechanism, and there are a variety of different latches available to suit various needs. One of the

Checking to see if the latch works correctly.

commonest types is the automatic latch. Whichever type of latch is chosen, it is important that both sides are lined up correctly, and this should be done whilst the gate is shut The latch can be then be fitted using the correct screws, which are usually supplied.

In some situations, such as a children's play area, it may be necessary for the gate to close automatically,

A spring closer fitted to a gate.

in which case a spring closer can be fitted that is fixed across the gate on the hinge side.

STILES

Stiles can offer an alternative form of access, and are normally used to provide access over a public right of way. They are also used where access is required for wildlife areas, and other places where animals may be kept, and the regular use of a gate may offer a possible escape route.

There are two types of stiles specified within the British Standards – the wide stile, which is designed to be climbed over by swinging the leg over sideways; and the narrow stile which is a step-over type. There is no statutory width or height for a stile, although the guidelines laid down by BS 5709: 2001 specify the following:

- There should be a maximum of two steps, with each step being a minimum width of 20cm (8in). On sloping ground, a platform of double the width of the step should be provided on the steepest side of the stile.
- The distance between the ground and the first step and also the distance between the top of the steps, should be no greater than 30cm (12in).
- Hand posts must be included.

Wide

This type of stile has a minimum width of 1.2m (4ft) and is built using the following method.

The posts should be 10cm (4in) square – one should be 1.7m (5ft 8in) in length; the other 46cm (18in) longer to allow for the handrail. Four 7.5×5cm (3×2in) rails are required of 1.3m (4ft 3in) in length, which allows for 7.5cm (3in) tenons on each end of the rails as these need to be stub mortised into the posts. Once this frame has been made up, it can be concreted into the ground with 76cm (30in) being set in the ground.

The step supports should then be constructed from 15×7.5cm (6×3in) square timber, consisting of two pieces of 66cm (26in) in length for the bottom step, and 46cm (18in) should be concreted in the ground. The top step supports should then be constructed, which should be 1m (3ft 4in) in length,

A wide stile, designed to be climbed over by swinging the leg sideways.

with 60cm (24in) concreted in the ground. The spacing of the posts should be 60–70cm (24–28in) which allows for some overhang when the steps, which should measure 90×20×5cm (3ft×8in×2in) are nailed to the supports.

Narrow

A good width for a narrow stile is approximately 60cm (24in), but this can be increased to 90cm (3ft)

if required. The construction methods used for the narrow stile are the same as those for the wide stile. To make a narrow stile, you will need two posts 10cm (4in) square, 1.9m (6ft 2in) in length, which allows for 76cm (30in) set in the ground; and two 7.5×5cm (3in×2in) rails, 76cm (30in) in length for a 60cm (24in) wide stile which allows for the tenons.

The specification for the top and bottom supports and steps is the same as for the wide stile.

A narrow stile, designed to be stepped over.

CHAPTER 6

Arches, Pergolas, Patio Overheads, Gazebos and Plant-Climbing Structures

All of the structures in this chapter can add height and interest to a garden, but they also have a practical purpose, whether it is to create a shady area to sit or walk in, an area for privacy, or as an individual feature that plants can climb up – or they can combine all of these purposes together.

ARCHES

An arch acts as a supporting structure for climbing plants, but also serves as an entrance, or to highlight and attract people towards a particular feature in the garden.

PERGOLAS

A pergola is a passageway of columns on which climbing plants are trained to grow, and in some cases they may have a trellis or some other type of climbing support attached to the sides. Pergolas can also be described as arbors as they are very similar in appearance to this type of structure that is created by trained trees, shrubs or climbers. However, in order to create this type of environment, a pergola-type structure is required to support climbers.

PATIO OVERHEADS OR LOGGIAS

The patio overhead, or loggia, is very similar in construction to a pergola. The primary difference between the two is that the overhead is usually situated over some type of patio or seating area such as a deck; and although plants can be grown up it, its main function is to give privacy and shade to its users. Although the top is of open construction similar to the pergola, the cross-pieces are sometimes

OPPOSITE, ABOVE: An ornate hexagonal pergola with partially trellised sides.

OPPOSITE, BELOW: A loggia acting as a protected passageway between two buildings.

RIGHT: An overhead built above a patio at the rear of a house.

closer together, and can run both along and upwards, giving a trellis effect.

A loggia is a covered arcade often attached to a building, open on one or more sides. It can be used as a storage area for such materials as firewood, a car port, or even as a protected walkway between buildings.

GAZEBOS

A gazebo is basically a shed, or similar building with no walls, although trellis fencing can be constructed between the uprights to support climbing plants

PLANT-CLIMBING STRUCTURES

In order for a climber to add visual impact to an area, it needs to be upright and in order for this to happen, it needs to be supported by some type of structure, which can be a trellis fence attached to a building or constructed between fence posts. Alternatively, a self-standing structure can be erected within a garden area, such as an obelisk.

PLACING OF STRUCTURES AND OTHER CONSIDERATIONS

Where the structure is to be constructed ultimately depends on what the structure is, and its intended use. For example, an obelisk's main function is to support plants away from a wall. However, it is also a decorative feature, which can be visually appealing with climbers growing up it, or in the winter when there is not as much growth, it can still enhance an area as a feature in its own right. This type of structure is ideal for adding height to a bed or border with low-lying plants. To create an impact, it is best to construct the obelisks in groups rather than on their own.

To give these structures greater visibility, attention should be paid to their colour. Nowadays, there are a variety of different coloured wood-stains available, so rather than choosing the traditional dark oak or mahogany, consideration should be given to colours such as green or gold, or even using a combination of colours such as dark oak for the main uprights and gold for the supports, which will help highlight the obelisks.

A gazebo with a sedum roof.

When looking at where to erect archways, their primary function must be considered, which is as an entrance to an area. Therefore they need to be situated between a fence, wall or hedge – anywhere where a visual entrance is required.

An archway, like an obelisk, is a structure that can be enhanced by climbing plants. You should, therefore, ensure there is sufficient planting space and depth of soil around the base of the archway, to enable plants to thrive.

To decide where to situate structures such as pergolas and gazebos, you first need to define how they are to be used. For example, the gazebo is mainly used as an area to sit in and view the garden, but it can also be an area for privacy and a place to shelter. Therefore, like the summerhouse, it is an extension of the living area, the main difference being that it is an open structure with no sides.

Bearing these points in mind, the exact location of the gazebo can be decided. Because of its open aspect, it needs to be an area that is not over exposed to the elements, or it may be necessary to erect some form of screen to provide protection. Another consideration is the view – as it is an

A willow weave obelisk.

A group of obelisks giving visual impact to a border.

Ensure there is sufficient soil around your structure for climbers to be planted.

view, neither should it be an area which interferes with the privacy of others.

Like the gazebo, the pergola can be used as a place to sit and relax, but it also offers protection from the weather. When planning this type of structure, the same factors should be taken into consideration as those for the gazebo.

If, on the other hand, it is to be used as a decorative structure to join up various sections of the garden, the proposed route needs to be decided upon as well as how it will fit in with the overall design of the garden. A pergola's visual appeal is increased by planting climbers to grow up the sides and over the top; therefore it needs to be built in an area where soil is accessible. The growth of plants over the pergola also helps block out noise, so a pergola grown at the boundary next to a road may offer a secluded walkway or sitting area, but could also act as a noise barrier for the rest of the garden.

However, as stated earlier, the main objective is to offer shade and privacy, and therefore this type of structure is traditionally built over a patio, seating area, or a deck. It can be either freestanding or attached to the side of a building, and the roofing either can be of open construction or have some form of roofing material attached to it, such as plastic corrugated sheeting or bamboo screening.

area where all four sides can be used, a central viewing area or a place where the majority of the sides can be utilized may be the most viable option. Privacy is also important – if this is to be used as a social area, you do not want it to be open to public

A good view of the garden is essential when siting any structure that is to be used as a social area.

CONSTRUCTION METHODS

Plant-Climbing Structures

These are probably the simplest structures to build. They can take the form of trellis fencing attached to walls or other structures, providing a framework for climbing plants to grow up. Alternatively, they can be freestanding structures such as obelisks, which will add interest and height to an open bed or border.

Obelisks

Obelisks add height to herbaceous borders and are an effective and ornamental way of supporting climbing plants such as sweet peas and clematis. During the summer months, the climbing plants will add colour and interest to the garden and during the winter the obelisk will act as a feature in its own right.

Designing and Making an Obelisk

The first decision to make is the height you require the structure to be and the maximum and minimum width, bearing in mind it is a pyramid. Other considerations will be what pattern the sides should be – diamond, horizontal or vertical plant supports, and what type of finial is required, if any, for the top of the structure. Also, the final colour of the obelisk should be considered – should it be just one colour, or would a combination of two colours be better?

Choice of Materials

The wood chosen should be pressure treated, as part of the structure will be below ground level and the obelisk itself will be exposed to the elements. Rough sawn pine is the best timber to use as it is inexpensive and the rough surface will allow the timber colorant/preservative to key more effectively, enabling the plants to grip the surface. A water-based, non-toxic timber product is best as it is the most user-friendly and fairly inexpensive.

Phillips head screws should be used to fix the main framework of the obelisk, as they hold the wood better than nails. Phillips head screws are easier to use than flat-headed ones as the screwdriver holds the screw more firmly. However, when fixing the batten, windowpane pins should be used as they are not holding any weight.

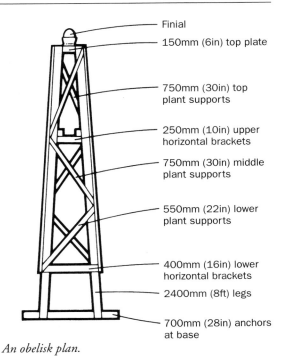

An obelisk plan.

Labels on diagram:
- Finial
- 150mm (6in) top plate
- 750mm (30in) top plant supports
- 250mm (10in) upper horizontal brackets
- 750mm (30in) middle plant supports
- 550mm (22in) lower plant supports
- 400mm (16in) lower horizontal brackets
- 2400mm (8ft) legs
- 700mm (28in) anchors at base

Building an Obelisk

When following these instructions, please refer to the diagram above.

Timber required for an obelisk 1.8m (6ft) high:

5×3.8cm (2×1½in) timber in the following lengths:
2.4m (8ft) × four upright legs
40cm (16in) × four lower horizontal brackets
25cm (10in) × four upper horizontal brackets
70cm (28in) × two anchors at the base
Total 5×3.8cm (2×1½in) timber required = 12.4m (40ft 8in)

2.5cm×19mm (1×¾in) in the following lengths:
76cm (30in) × eight top two sets of plant supports
55cm (22in) × four lower set of plant supports
Total 2.5cm×19mm (1×¾in) timber required

Also required:
A plank 15cm (6in) square, and approximately 3.8cm (1½in) thick for the top plate
A 15×10cm (6×4in) pine acorn finial

A single obelisk.

Tips for Constructing an Obelisk

The timber should all be cut to size and treated with the wood preservative/colorant before putting it together. For this type of construction, it is best to use Phillips head wood screws. After the wood stain has dried, construct two side panels first, to the design shown in the diagram on page 99. Once these have been built, they need to be joined together, using the lower and upper brackets and then attach-ing both the top and lower plant supports. Now that the main frame has been erected, the two anchors can be attached to the sides right at the bottom of the main frame legs. After this has been done then the top plate

should be fixed to the top of the main frame, and then the finial can be attached by screwing from underneath the top plate and into the base of the finial.

Once all the parts of the obelisk have been joined together, it can be erected. In order to do this, place the obelisk in position and mark round it with an aerosol spray to ascertain the diameter of the hole to be dug. Remove the obelisk and dig a hole approximately 50cm (20in) deep, depending on the size of the structure and how open or protected the site is. It is not a good idea to concrete the obelisk into position, as this will prevent plants from growing up it. One of the main reasons why anchors are fitted is so that the soil can be firmed round the base, and the anchors will hold the structure in position.

Once the obelisk has been erected, the climbers can be planted. It is recommended to plant two climbers per obelisk, which should be positioned opposite each other on either side, and then tied in position so that they will grow around the structure.

Alternatively the main framework can be constructed as above, and then trellis fencing can be cut to size and attached. On the other hand, you can make your own trellis design, or even attach the battens in a different pattern to that described. This is all a matter of personal choice, bearing in mind the overall effect required, and how it matches in with the rest of the garden.

Other Types of Obelisk

As well as the obelisk framework described above, pre-assembled obelisks in various designs can be purchased. Also, simpler forms of obelisk can be constructed, consisting of three rustic poles tied at the top with garden twine in a wigwam formation and fixed into the ground in the same way as the other types of obelisk. Top and bottom supports can be added to the wigwam fencing using a basketweave pattern, or bamboo or wicker fencing can be attached between the supports. However, probably the most basic type of obelisk is made by hammering a single rustic pole into the ground, and training something such as a climbing rose to grow up it.

Other Plant-Climbing Structures

As well as the obelisks, which are freestanding, you can also erect trellis fencing to buildings or walls, and then attach climbers so that they help to disguise the brick or stone work, whilst using the trellis as a support.

Do not attach trelliswork directly to the surface, as a gap is required behind for the climbing plants to wrap around it. Fix timber strips 3.8cm (1½in) square to the wall. They should be the same length as the trellis that is to be erected. The first should be fixed just above the damp course, and the others spaced approximately 90cm (3ft) apart. The final piece of wood should be as near to the top of the trellis as possible – at least within 15cm (6in). The timber strips should be pre-drilled and attached to the wall using screws. In the case of masonry surfaces, the wooden strips need to be held in place and the holes marked. The holes can then be drilled and rawlplugs inserted. When attaching the strips to the surface,

always check that they are level, because if they are not, they may not be in line with the battens on the trellis, which can cause problems when erecting the trellis fence.

Once all the wooden strips are in place, the trellis fencing can be attached using galvanized nails. However, where surfaces need regular maintenance, it may be best to use screws to attach the trellis to the wood so that they can easily be taken out if the trellis needs to be removed.

An alternative method, which is especially useful for large and heavy trelliswork, is to attach hinges to one end of the trellis and then screw the screws are undone, so that access can be gained to the surface behind. The width that the trellis fence can be opened is dependent on how tight to the wall the climber is. Therefore when using this method, it is

ABOVE: *Trellis fencing attached to a wall in order to give support to climbing plants.*

RIGHT: *A rustic pole wigwam obelisk.*

101

best to plant any climbers 46–60cm (18–24in) away from the wall. When planting, lean them towards the wall and attach to the bottom of the trellis

Gazebos

Gazebos, like many other wooden structures in this book, can be erected either using self-assembly kits, or built to your own design. A self-built structure can be either quite complex, such as an oak-beamed obelisk with a solid shingle roof, or something much simpler, such as a softwood post gazebo with a trellis roof.

Planting a climber so that it leans towards the wall.

A Trellis Roof Gazebo

This is probably the simplest form of gazebo to build. It is constructed using four 7.5cm (3in) square posts that should stand about 2m (7ft) out of the ground. It is usually sufficient to use metal fence posts for this size of structure and therefore the posts purchased need to be the same length as the desired height. However, if the structure is to be constructed in an area that is prone to strong winds, or the gazebo is to be of heavier construction detail than shown below, it may be wise to concrete the posts into the ground. If this method is to be used then 60cm (24in) needs to be added on, because this is the amount of the post to be buried.

Once the size of the posts and the method by which they are to be held in position has been decided upon, the length of the horizontal rails that are going to connect the tops of the posts needs to be considered. The best way to do this is to mark your favoured size for the gazebo using pegs and lines on the ground first, and these can then be moved either inwards or outwards, until you have the desired size. Measure along the string line on all sides to establish the length of the rails required. The rail length will be longer than their final size because they are fitted between the posts using a tenon and mortise joint. This measurement does not take into consideration the width of the posts, but it does allow for the tenon, which will be 5cm (2in) in length.

The rails themselves need to be 7.5×5cm (3×2in) timber, and as a general guideline, this type of gazebo is best as a square construction. Each side should be a minimum of 1.8m (6ft) for comfort and a maximum of 3m (10ft) for safety. Once the posts have been set in position and the rails fitted, measure and cut eight diagonal braces that can be secured in place by nailing.

Now that the framework is set in position, it is time to construct the roof. This should consist of four 7.5×5cm (3×2in) rafters, the length of which depends on the size of the gazebo. When cutting the rafters to size, allow for 7.5cm (3in) overhang then mark and cut a bird's mouth so that they fit over the rails. Allow enough length at the top of the rafters to cut a 5cm (2in) tenon. The tenons should be set into a mortised central block of wood measuring 10cm (4in) square and is approximately 20cm (8in) wide,

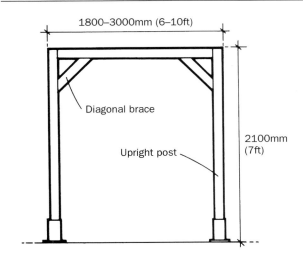

Construction of a gazebo framework.

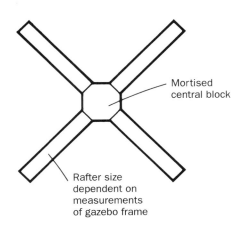

Construction of a gazebo roof.

which allows enough room to attach a pointed finial. The roof rafters should be nailed into position and the tenon and mortise joints glued and nailed also to ensure a strong fitting.

The final stage in this construction process is to cut the pre-formed trellis to fit the roof sections and nail it into position. If necessary, the trellis can also be fitted to some of the sides to provide privacy or give protection from the wind.

Arches

An arch can be bought as a ready-made structure, which either can be a stand-alone feature, or may form part of a package, for example matching fencing and planters. Like gazebos, very complex and expensive structures can be built, but it is quite feasible to build something much less complicated that serves the same purpose either as an entrance, or to highlight a feature.

An archway is a fairly simple structure to build, and there are two basic designs to choose from when building an arch from wood – either a flat-topped, or an apex arch. In addition to these, there is also the round-topped or gothic arch. Although these designs are often found constructed from wrought iron, prefabricated wooden types are also available. It is possible to construct this type of arch from scratch, but it is a fairly difficult task to undertake and the

right wood and specialist tools need to be used. Therefore, if you wish to include this type of design in your garden, the easiest option is to purchase a prefabricated structure.

If designing and constructing your own arch from wood, one of the simplest structures to build is a

A flat-topped pergola arch.

A rustic apex arch.

trellis arch, which is made using similar construction techniques as when erecting a gazebo. However this is not the only way to construct an archway, and probably one of the most effective and popular types are the ones made using rustic poles, because of their natural appearance and appropriateness for a variety of landscape designs.

A Rustic Arch

These are constructed using poles with, or without, bark and can be purchased directly from a timber yard or builder's merchant. The advantage with the poles without bark on is that they are usually available pressure treated, whereas poles that still have their bark will be untreated, although this type of timber has a more natural appearance and is invariably cheaper. You can process it yourself from pruned branches in your own garden, as long as they are straight and of a sufficient diameter. If an untreated pole is used, the bottom layer of bark should be removed, which will be 46–60cm (18–24in) in length. The bottoms of the prepared poles must then stand overnight in a bucket of wood preservative. The length of the area to be treated is dependent upon how much of the pole is to be buried in the ground. Once the bottoms of the poles have been treated, several coats of polyurethane varnish should be applied to seal the wood, which will give overall protection.

When designing an arch, either of rustic construction or from other materials, one of the main considerations is the width between the poles. This is especially important where the arch is to be used for access purposes. If wheelchair access is required, at least 1.2m (4ft) needs to be allowed, but even if this is not a major consideration, the archway should be wide enough for two people walking side by side to pass under comfortably, or if it is to be used to highlight a feature or set of features, it should be large enough to accommodate them. Once the width and design of the arch has been decided, the amount of timber required can be worked out.

An apex rustic arch will comprise the following timbers, although this may vary according to individual design. When selecting timber for any type of rustic structure, as well as selecting the right length of timber, you must also ensure that it is all of a similar diameter, as this will make the construction process easier, and will also produce a neater, more professional looking end product.

Four poles are needed to form the main frame. When these are sunk in the ground there should be at least 1.8m (6ft) above ground level, so the poles themselves need to be at least 2m (7ft) in length. The poles are joined together in pairs to form the sides of the arch – again the depth is dependent on personal preference. They are attached with horizontal poles in a ladder effect – this can range from three to five side poles, according to the spacing used. Four poles are also required to form the apex of the roof, allowing a 30cm (12in) overhang on each side. You will need a top beam (pole) to join the apexes together, and a central pole to strengthen the apex section, cut to the same length as the horizontal poles. Now that the timber has been cut to size, you need to make sure that all the components fit together. The best way to do this is to lay all the

Laying out the framework for the arch in order to check that all the parts have been cut and fit in place.

pieces out on a flat surface and check that the right number of pieces has been cut, that the design is as required and that they will fit in position correctly.

The two side frames should be constructed by nailing the horizontal poles between the vertical poles, and it good practice to lay both frames next to each other when carrying out this task, to ensure that both sets of poles are spaced at exactly the same distance apart. Once the side frames have been constructed, space the panels at the correct distance apart, hold in place using scrap wood as braces and nail across the frames at the top and at the bottom. The apex section can now be put together and should be nailed to the top of the frame with the horizontal poles nailed between it.

Now that the arch has been constructed, cut a piece of wood the same length as the width between the poles and another the same length as the depth between the front and back poles. These two pieces of wood can now be used as spacers to locate the four holes for the frame.

The holes should then be dug and the arch put in position. The posts should be checked that they are straight and level with a spirit level. Also check that the base is straight using a builder's square. Once this has all been checked the posts can be concreted in, using the same methods as when concreting in a fence post. The braces should be left attached to the arch until the concrete has set, after which they can be removed.

Pergolas

There are two common types of pergola. The traditional pergola consists of straight cross-beams, spaced evenly across and attached directly on top of two main beams. The other, more ornate, type of design is the oriental pergola where the beams and cross-beams are fitted into notches cut into the main beam, and all of the beams are either bevelled or curved at the ends.

A traditional pergola design.

There are two variations to these designs – one of these is to construct a pergola from rustic poles using the traditional design, and is usually associated with climbing roses. The other is to build a lean-to pergola that is attached to a wall, and either traditional or oriental designs can be used

A Traditional Pergola

The traditional freestanding pergola is probably the easier of the designs to construct and one of the strongest. As stated previously, one of the pergola's main functions is to support climbing plants, which will mean that eventually the whole structure will be covered by climbers. Therefore, when choosing wood for this type of structure, it is best to use pressure-treated rough sawn timber, the reason being that plants will grip to the surface better, and because the plants will cover all the structure eventually, the pressurized treatment will give added protection to the wood. Bearing this in

mind, it is always a good idea to treat the structure with an additional coat of preservative after it has been constructed.

When planning the pergola, as with all structures, it is best to mark out the size and shape of it first on the ground. When considering where to put a pergola, bear in mind that it tends to work better as part of an overall design rather than as a stand-alone feature. When deciding on the exact measurements of the pergola, you need to consider the distance between the upright posts, which can vary depending on individual needs and designs. However, the recommended lengthwise measurement between posts is 1.8m (6ft), as this is the standard measurement of this type of panel and will allow prefabricated trellis panels to be fixed between them. As a general rule, it is best to decide whether you require side panels on the pergola before putting in the posts as it is easier to install them as the posts are being erected and the

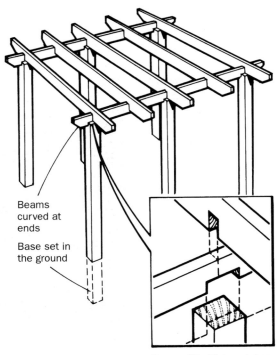

Beams
curved at
ends

Base set in
the ground

Beams fitted into notches

An oriental pergola design.

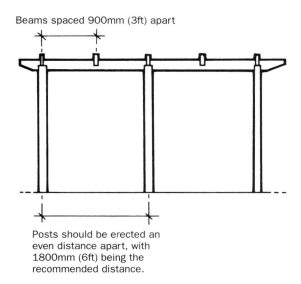

Beams spaced 900mm (3ft) apart

Posts should be erected an even distance apart, with 1800mm (6ft) being the recommended distance.

Spacing of posts for a pergola.

very strong footings, and concrete should be the chosen option. In more sheltered areas, for shorter structures, or where the ground is harder, fence spikes can be used. The advantage of using them is that they are quicker and easier to install, and also you can plant climbers nearer to the posts, as there is no concrete in the way.

Once all the posts have been erected, the top beams need to be attached to the top of the posts. In instances where two beams are attached to the same post, they should be joined half-and-half, and 'L'-shaped brackets which are secured by screws should be used for this purpose.

The two sets of posts and top beams are joined together using cross-pieces nailed to the top of the frame starting at one end, and should be spaced approximately 90cm (3ft) apart. The cross-pieces can be either flush with the top beams, or can overhang by approximately 15cm (6in) on either side.

construction principles used for putting up a panel fence can be followed.

Because the pergola is used as a frame for climbing plants, the final size of the plants should be taken into consideration. It is estimated that a climbing plant will extend at least 7.5cm (3in), and on average about 13cm (5in). Therefore, when planning the width and height of your structure, allow an additional 7.5cm (3in) either side for path widths and an additional 13cm (5in) for height, with the ideal clear headroom being 2m (7ft) from the underside of the woodwork.

Now that the location and size of the pergola has been decided, the next step is to mark out where the posts are to be positioned, which should be done by using pegs and string to form an outline, ensuring that the base is square. The position of the four corner posts can then be marked out. Once this has been done, measure from the posts in order to locate where any inner posts are to be erected. The posts, side beams and cross-pieces for this type of construction should be a minimum of 10cm (4in) square and can be concreted into the ground or post spikes can be used. The fixing method used is dependent upon the height and location of the pergola. High and exposed structures, or those on soft ground will need

Top beams attached to the top of the posts half-and-half and secured with 'L'-shaped brackets.

107

Patio Overheads and Loggias

There are a wide range of materials that can be used to cover patio overheads and loggias.

Corrugated Panels

Corrugated panels come in a range of materials, but plastic is the most usual for this type of construction. The reason for this is that it gives protection from the weather whilst letting light in. It is a lightweight material that will not add too much weight to the top of the structure and therefore there will be little strain on the joists. It is also quite a strong material and will stand up to the various extremes of weather, including snow, heavy rain or strong wind. It is recommended that corrugated panels are fixed to slanted roof frames, or that flat roof frames are erected so that they have a slight fall, in order that water and melting snow can run off. To attach the corrugated panels to the frame pilot, holes should be drilled at the edge of the sheets and attached to the frame using screws and fibre washers.

Woven Reed and Bamboo Sheeting

This type of material can add a tropical look to the structure, provides dense shade and can give some protection from the rain, although a heavy downfall will come through. It is not the most suitable material to use in areas where there is heavy snow, as prolonged snow covering could damage and rot it. When attaching either the woven reed or bamboo sheeting to the frame, galvanized wire staples should be used and wooden strips nailed on top of the sheeting to the framework, including the cross-timbers, to help hold the sheeting tightly in position, which in turn will help prevent wind damage.

Shade Materials

Shade materials can be bought from horticultural suppliers, as they are also used to give protection to crops from the sun's rays. It is available in various densities, which provide 20–90 percent shade and is usually either green or black in colour. Like the woven reed and bamboo sheeting, it will only give limited protection from rain. However it is fairly rot resistant and will last for many years, but may stretch if covered with snow for prolonged periods. It is attached by stretching so it is taught over the frame-

work and then stapling the edges. Once this has been done, nail wooden strips around the framework on top of where the shade material has been stapled to ensure it is held in position.

Spaced Laths

Spaced laths consist of either 5×2.5cm (2×1in) or 5cm (2in) square lengths of timber attached to the roof framework and spaced according to the amount of shade required. This is easy to install and is visually attractive. It will give only limited rain protection, but will cope well with heavy snow.

Trellis Panels

A very simple method, consisting of attaching trellis panels to the roof framework which will give some shade and some privacy and is visually appealing, but will give little protection from the weather

Overheads or loggias are constructed using the same techniques as those used when erecting a pergola. However, as these structures have to bear more weight because of the roof construction, it is not recommended that post spikes are used – the posts should be concreted in instead. Where the posts are to be attached to decking or another hard surface, metal post anchors should be used.

Because of the weight of the roof structure, it will necessary to brace the overhead. This is done using 10×2.5cm (4×1in) or 15×2.5cm (6×1in) braces with ends cut at 45-degree angles. They are used in pairs and nailed to the post, so that they are attached to the supporting beam of the upright at a ninety-degree angle.

In some situations instead of being freestanding, one edge of the overhead or loggia can be attached to a wall, and in order to do this a ledger beam 10×5cm (4×2in) will be necessary. On a building wall, the ledger beam can be fitted directly under the fascia board, and this can be used as a guideline to ensure that the board is level. It is fixed into position using coach screws that should be spaced every 1.2m (4ft), penetrating through the fascia board and into the solid timber underneath.

The ledger beam can also be attached directly onto the wall. If this method is used, you first need to measure from the base of the wall, up to where the top of the ledger will be. Once this has been done,

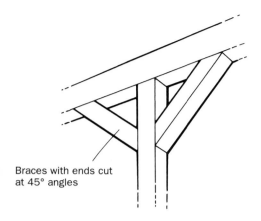

Braces with ends cut at 45° angles

Bracing the overhead.

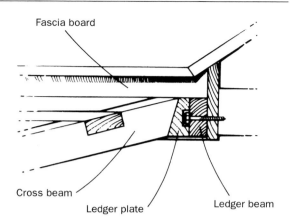

Fascia board

Cross beam

Ledger plate

Ledger beam

Attaching the ledger beam to the fascia board.

place a straight-edged piece of wood the length of the wall, check with a spirit level and mark a horizontal line with chalk along the top of the wood. Drill holes in the ledger board large enough for the bolts to be spaced 1.2m (4ft) apart. Hold the ledger board so that the top edge is level with the chalk line, and then mark the position of the bolts through the pre-drilled holes. Once the holes have been marked, remove the board and drill into the wall to a depth of 11.5cm (4½in) with a 3.5cm (1⅜in) diameter masonry bit then attach the ledger to the wall using 16.5cm×16mm (6½×⅝in) anchor bolts.

The cross-pieces can now be attached to the ledger beam by nailing them directly on top. Alternatively, grooves can be cut into the ledger beam for the cross-pieces to sit into and nailed into position. This method can also be used for sloping roofs, as the groove can be cut at an angle to accommodate the cross-beam. The free-standing upright posts with the supporting beam on top should then be positioned lower than the ledger beam – the exact height of this is determined by the fall you wish the overhead to have. When attaching the cross-pieces, an angled groove should be cut in the supporting beam, so that the cross-pieces fit flush within the groves, and are then nailed into position.

Alternatively, ledger plates can be fitted to the sides of the beams, and these can be either angled or straight, depending on what type of overhead is required.

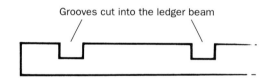

Grooves cut into the ledger beam

Attaching the cross-pieces.

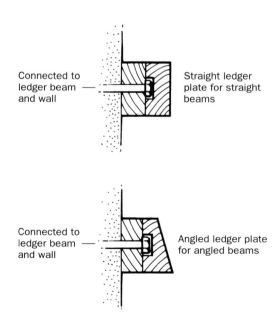

Connected to ledger beam and wall

Straight ledger plate for straight beams

Connected to ledger beam and wall

Angled ledger plate for angled beams

Fitting ledger plates.

A traditional oak gazebo with a shingle roof and a trellis fence on the sides, both for privacy and to enable climbers to grow up it.

ADAPTATIONS

Walls

Instead of the upright posts on pergolas, overheads, gazebos, or arches coming straight out of the ground, a low wall can be built and posts attached to the top of the wall using metal post sockets. The wall can be built from brick, stone, or any other suitable material. Whatever material is chosen, it is essential that the top of the wall is level and wide enough to enable you to attach the post sockets. If a brick wall is built, this is usually built as a double wall and capped with full bricks across the top.

In situations where a planter is required at the base of a structure, a double-sided wall can be built and filled with soil for planting climbers and other plants that will eventually cover the wall. It is important when constructing a planter from a solid material that adequate drainage is incorporated, otherwise the plants will not survive. If this type of construction is used then the posts can be concreted in the centre of the planters.

Plant Supports

The trellis has already been mentioned throughout this book as a method of supporting plants. A trellis on a structure has a decorative as well as a practical purpose. However, there are alternative methods, including both wire and mesh, which either can be galvanized or plastic coated. When using wire or mesh, its purpose is not to be seen but to serve as a plant support framework.

Both the wire and the mesh are usually attached to the outer side of the upright posts and secured in place using staples. The wires are attached horizontally across the posts and are spaced approximately 30cm (12in) apart. The wire mesh is stretched to fit across the framework. The main difference between these two methods of support is that because the mesh is solid, it also can act as a barrier if required, whereas the wire does not form a barrier on its own but it is less obtrusive to the naked eye.

CHAPTER 7

Planters, Raised Borders, Cold Frames and Compost Bins

PLANTERS AND RAISED BORDERS

The main differences between a planter and a raised border are that a raised border is usually larger and a fixed structure.

Planters

A planter, as the name suggests, is somewhere that plants can be grown. They can vary in size from small ones that can be lifted by one person, right up to those that need to be moved by some form of mechanical means such as a forklift truck. Planters can be used in groups or individually and can serve the following purposes.

To Add Colour
The planter itself can be painted in bright colours to enhance an area, but is mainly used for planting up with seasonal bedding, which can make an area more appealing and welcoming.

Privacy, Shelter and Disguising Unattractive Features
Planting up taller plants or installing trelliswork at the back of a planter for climbing plants can provide

Planters filled with colourful plants to brighten up an area.

a temporary screen or windbreak on a patio and such like. It can be used to hide unsightly features such as meter boxes, bins, or any other feature that spoils the general appearance of the area.

As well as using plants to hide certain features, the planters themselves can be used. For example, they can be positioned on top of manhole covers, but if used for this purpose it may be wise to use lighter or wheeled containers in case access is required.

Raised Borders

As it is a fixed structure, careful planning is required when deciding on where a raised border is to be placed and how it is going to be constructed. Raised borders serve the same purposes as planters but also have the following uses.

As a Soil Retainer

In some cases it may be necessary to build a retaining structure in order to hold back areas where the soil level is higher than any hard surfaces or lawns.

To Make Gardening Easier

Raised planters are ideal for wheelchair users or people who have back problems. If intended for such purposes, ensure that it is built to a suitable height. The width needs to be such that all of the planter can

be gardened. In order to achieve this, it needs to be accessible from all sides.

This type of planter can also be used for the 'no-dig' method of vegetable gardening, which basically consists of filling it with a suitable mixture of compost and soil, and then planting as you would a traditional vegetable plot. Once the crop has finished and everything is harvested, the planter can be topped up with a compost and soil mix and there is no need to dig the plot.

Other Uses of Planters and Raised Beds

As well as using these structures for plants or vegetables, they can be used for ponds, wetland planting, ericaceous plants, rockeries or any other types of planting that require specialist types of soil or conditions that cannot be provided within the confines of the garden.

CONSTRUCTING A PLANTER

It is a relatively simple process to construct rectangular, square, apex or even hexagonal freestanding planters. The square and rectangular planters are probably the most common types and can be adapted for a variety of different uses, and, like the apex planter, are ideal for positioning in corners.

Planters with trellis fencing used to soften a building.

A pond in a raised bed framework.

Hexagonal planters can add a different dimension to a relatively straight area because of their shape.

The overall size of the planter is very much dependent on what it is to be used for, and where it is to be positioned. It is worth considering constructing a number of smaller, more manageable planters rather than one large one, because with all types of designs, the planters can be positioned close together to form a larger planter, or they can be positioned in such a way as to form different designs and patterns.

Once the size and shape of the planter has been decided, the next step is the overall look, in other words, what type of material is going to be used on the outside. Again, this depends on personal preference and how it is going to fit with the overall design of the garden. There are many types of materials

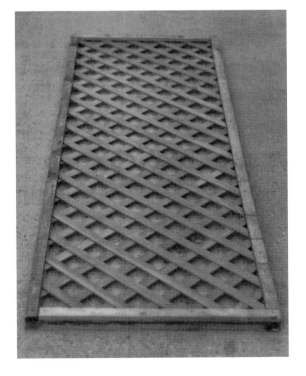

Lattice panels, which can be cut to size and fitted onto the sides of planters to give a decorative effect.

Apex, hexagonal and square-shaped planters.

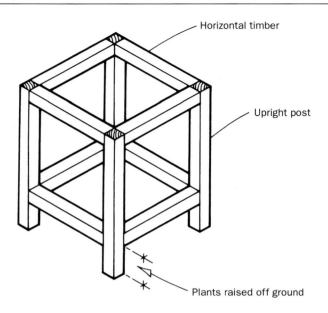

A frame for a square planter.

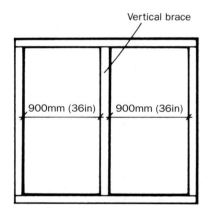

Fitting vertical braces for larger planters.

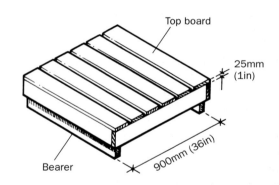

Construction of the base.

available for this purpose, including the wood off old pallets, or, at the other end of the scale, cedar or oak panels. If the timber from old pallets is used, it is important that any old nails and staples are removed, and that it is treated with an appropriate wood preservative and stain. For a more decorative effect, it may be worth considering attaching lattice panels on top of your chosen cladding.

The interior lining of the planter is another consideration, because if the soil is in constant contact with the wood there is a greater risk of it rotting quickly. Also, without a liner, soil and water may seep through and spoil the appearance of the planter. Polythene sheeting is often used for this purpose, however, as is it is non-permeable the compost can become waterlogged, which is not beneficial for the plants and also it may cause unpleasant odours if the compost is stagnant. Therefore the best type of material to use is woven polypropylene, which is traditionally used on the ground as a weed suppressant. The advantage of this product is that it is permeable so that it will allow excess water to seep out, but also will give some protection to the inside of the container whilst holding the soil in place. However, there is a disadvantage to using this material – as it is permeable, there may be a slight seepage of water through the sides of the container and this can cause staining. One way of preventing this is to attach polythene around the inner sides before lining it with the woven sheeting.

Once the materials for the planter itself have been chosen, you can decide if any plant support system needs to be incorporated into the design, and this can include trellis fencing attached to the back of the planter. For planters that are going to be placed so as to be viewed from all angles, an obelisk or similar structure within the centre of the planter may be a viable option.

Now that the design of the planter has been decided, the next step is to construct a frame, which can be made using rough sawn timber 7.5cm (3in) square, the amount required depending upon individual designs, although the method of construction process will remain the same. For example, in order to construct a square planter measuring 90cm (3ft) square, you will need four pieces of timber 90cm (3ft) in length for the corner posts, and eight pieces of timber 75cm (30in) in length. Attach four pieces between the corner posts at the top, and four pieces at the bottom in order to form a square frame. It is best to join the framework together using screws and waterproof wood glue. For planters with sides of more than 1.8m (6ft) in length, vertical mid-braces should be fitted between the frame approximately 90cm (3ft) apart, otherwise the weight of the soil within the planter may cause the boards to bow.

Now that the framework has been built, the base can be constructed from 15×2.5cm (6×1in) boards, screwed to the base of the frame. Fit timber bearers 90cm (3ft) square to the base. Depending on the size of the planters, the bearers should be fitted approximately 90cm (3ft) apart, so that they can support the weight of the planter. It is important that the base of the planter is raised off the ground to enable water to drain freely.

The next stage is to attach the cladding to the sides of the planter, which should be nailed into position along the framework. If shorter lengths of timber are used, such as pallet laths, extra mid-braces may need to be fitted so that the cladding can be fixed into position. If the structure is made of boards rather than whole panels, you should start at the bottom and work upwards, nailing into position.

If trellis fencing is going to be used, this can be attached on the outside. If they are prefabricated panels, cut them to the size required and remove the bottom two or three horizontal cross-pieces, leaving the vertical pieces that can then be attached at the rear of the planter using screws. Alternatively, you can build your own trellis, designed to suit your needs. In order to do this 3.8cm×12mm (1½×½in) timber strips should be used.

The final stage is to attach the liner inside the container and this is normally done using a heavy-duty staple gun.

The planter is now ready for filling with compost and planting. However, before doing this, it may be

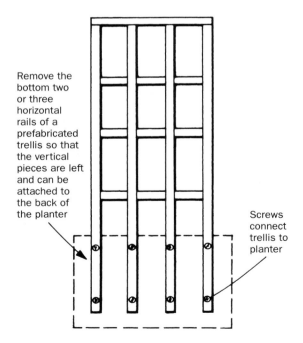

Remove the bottom two or three horizontal rails of a prefabricated trellis so that the vertical pieces are left and can be attached to the back of the planter

Screws connect trellis to planter

Attaching trellis fencing to the back of the planter.

worth considering attaching castors to the base. This is important for large and heavy planters that are situated on hard-standing areas that may have to be regularly moved.

CONSTRUCTING A RAISED BED

Crib Walling

Crib walling is a method used to retain large heights of earth and dates back to the late Iron Age where they were constructed from layers of horizontal timbers spiked together, filled with soil and rubble and then faced with undressed stone.

The principal remains unchanged and in fact some conservation societies still retain bankings using the traditional method. However, for modern landscapes, structurally engineered walling systems have been developed that are both aesthetically pleasing and retain large amounts of earth. They are available in both wood and concrete; the wooden ones are made from softwood, and consist of timber beams of 50cm–2m (20in–6ft 8in) in length, which lock together to form the crib.

They should be laid into the banking at an approximately 10-degree batter (angle), but this can vary depending on the situation. The cribs can vary in depth but are usually about 1.2m (4ft). It is essential that the base is firm and a hardcore base should be laid before installing. After each layer has been laid it should be filled with graded stone, and if planting is required the front 46cm (18in) should be filled with top soil. Once this has been done, the next layer should be laid and this process continued for each layer until the crib wall is built. The infilling of graded stone is an important aspect, as this is what counteracts any soil movement, and allows water to drain through. Because this system is very free draining, the soil can become very dry, which makes it important to choose drought-resistant plants.

This type of system has an unlimited life expectancy if done correctly. Bearing in mind its purpose, it is imperative that the crib wall manufacturer or a civil engineer is consulted before this work is undertaken. The reason for this being that there are many types of crib walls available that will suit a variety of situations and the installation of these may vary according to what system is chosen. Therefore these instructions should be used as a guide only when considering this type of retaining wall system.

Log Walling

Traditionally, log walls were built from elm, which did not rot in wet situations. Now this is no longer available, it has been replaced by standardized, machine-made, pressure-treated softwood logs, and in normal situations these will last up to twenty years.

A crib wall.

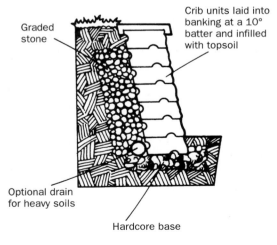

Graded stone

Crib units laid into banking at a 10° batter and infilled with topsoil

Optional drain for heavy soils

Hardcore base

Laying a crib wall.

A horizontal log-retaining wall used in a wildlife area.

They are available in different diameters and lengths, but 10cm (4in) diameter logs are the most popular type used in landscape construction, especially for vertical log-retaining walls. Natural or rustic logs can also be used for log walls although they will not last as long. If they are to be buried or concreted in, it is advisable to remove any bark from the base and then soak in wood preservative overnight. Any bare ends should be treated with wood preservative. It is also a good idea with untreated logs to apply a coat of clear outdoor wood varnish to give some protection.

Both natural and prepared logs have their advantages and disadvantages. The appeal of natural logs is their natural and rustic look, which makes them the preferred choice for cottage and wildlife gardens, conservation areas and so on. They are also relatively cheap and can usually be purchased in bulk direct from a timber yard.

However there are two disadvantages with this type of log. The first one is that the lack of pressure treatment may shorten their life, especially where they are used in damp situations. The other disadvantage is that because they are a natural product, uniformity may be a problem in respect their diameter and how straight they are. Therefore, it is essential that you specify to your supplier what purpose

you require them for, and give a guide to the diameter you require, which can be anything between 10cm (4in) and 20cm (8in) for this type of construction, depending on individual specifications. For instance, a larger diameter log may be required for a retaining wall, where there is significant soil pressure, or it may be the case that a smaller or larger diameter log is chosen so that it is in proportion with the landscape structure and the rest of the garden.

The advantages of machine-prepared logs are that they are pressure treated, which will prolong their life, and it is also possible to predict their anticipated lifespan. They are uniform in diameter and straight, which makes the construction process a lot easier and means that when they are fitted into position they should fit tightly together, leaving virtually no gaps. This type of log is readily available from most timber yards and suppliers of landscaping products. As well as the rounded logs, they can also be purchased as half logs, either individually or in log rolls. However, full logs are best suited for purposes of soil retention.

Half logs are mainly used for borders in their log roll form, as it is easier to install. They are not particularly suitable for retaining soil but can be used as a decorative edging for a border or where a raised border is constructed from concrete blocks or other

*A machine-prepared
vertical log wall.*

material that is not visually appealing. In these situations, they can be used to disguise the wall, which then gives the structures the appearance of a log wall border.

Log rolls are normally available in 2m (7ft) lengths and various depths They are attached together using galvanized wire, and can have a ten-year guarantee, but this is dependent on where they are purchased. Another big advantage of using log rolls if they are used to disguise a wall is that they can be easily removed and replaced.

Both the machine-prepared full log and half logs are more health and safety friendly than natural logs, especially when used vertically as they have a chamfered edge that can help prevent serious injury if someone like a small child falls on them. Their main disadvantage is their appearance, which looks manufactured. However, there are many different wood stains available that can help to give them a more natural appearance if this is required.

Constructing a Vertical Log Wall

When installing a vertical log wall you first need to mark out where the wall is going to be, which can be done using a string line for straight lines and marker paint or a hosepipe for curved walls. Once this has been done, a trench needs to be dug, and for logs of up to 1.2m (4ft) high, 46cm (18in) needs to be

buried and an additional 30cm (12in) should added to the depth of the trench for drainage. For log walls higher than 46cm (18in), one third of the length of the post needs to be buried, and again an additional 30cm (12in) should be dug for drainage. The width of the trench is dependent on the diameter of the logs used, but at least 15cm (6in) should be allowed either side of the post. Also, if the wall is to be installed next to an existing raised soil area there needs to be a gap of at least 46cm (18in) between the banking and edge of the trench to allow adequate working space to install the logs correctly.

When the trench has been dug, fill the bottom 30cm (12in) with coarse gravel or rubble, which will act as a drainage layer. Where the outer edge of the logs are going to be, a line needs to be set out if a straight log wall is to be erected; if the wall is to be curved then a hosepipe can be used. The logs can now be put in position and concreted in. The tops of the posts can either be checked with a spirit level, or, alternatively, they can be set in the ground at different heights in order to form various patterns.

If using rustic or natural logs, they also can be laid so that all the tops are level, or if a curved design is required, the logs should be set in the ground, so that they are higher than the required height. The design required can be marked on the logs using chalk, and then cut along the chalk line using a chainsaw.

When all the logs have been erected, allow the concrete to set for at least forty-eight hours, and then fix woven polypropylene sheeting to the inside of the posts before backfilling with soil.

Constructing a Horizontal Log Wall

A horizontal log wall gives a different effect to the vertical method. It consists of logs laid horizontally and the uprights concreted in at 1.5m (5ft) centres. The main disadvantage with this method is that because of the way it is constructed, only straight runs can be built whereas the vertical log wall method is suitable for virtually any shape. However, one advantage is that because the posts are bolted to the uprights, if they rot, break or are damaged in any way they can be fairly easily replaced by undoing the bolts – although if one of the uprights breaks this will affect the whole run.

For this type of retaining wall, it is best to use machine-prepared logs rather than natural ones, especially if it is going to be several logs high, because the logs are laid in sections similar to a panel fence, and in order for each section to match in and all of the logs to run in straight runs, logs that are straight and uniform in diameter need to be used; although rustic or natural logs can be used quite effectively as a low support for a border, either one or two logs in height. When using machine-prepared logs, the horizontal logs should be 10cm (4in) and the uprights 15cm (6in) in diameter. Also, in situations where it is extremely damp, or there is substantial soil pressure, it may be worth considering using thicker uprights or pre-drilled ones made from a stronger, more rot-resistant material such as concrete, because, as stated before, once the uprights have rotted or broken, the whole run is affected.

The horizontals should be drilled so that they can be bolted to the uprights. However, it is important to ensure that there is an overhang of at least 30cm (12in) when they are connected to the uprights, as this provides enough room for the next upright posts to be erected in the run. Start at the bottom, mark on the uprights where it is to be attached, drill the first set of holes for the first horizontal log and attach with bolts. Repeat this process for the remainder of the logs. It is important when erecting this type of retaining wall that the concrete around the uprights has been given sufficient time to set before drilling into it, otherwise this will weaken the structure.

Rustic or natural logs they can be erected using the same methods. However, as only a low wall is being constructed, an easier method is to drive wooden

A sloping vertical log wall created by setting the logs in the ground at different heights.

stakes of approximately 10cm (4in) into the ground at either the back or the side of the logs. The logs can then be attached to these by hammering in galvanized nails at an angle.

Log Block Walls

A raised bed can also be created by using natural logs of 15cm (6in) and 30cm (12in) in diameter and 30cm (12in) and 60cm (24in) in length. The sawn side or diameter of the log is the facing side, and the wall is built in a similar way to a dry stone wall, in that the logs need to lean slightly into the banking or soil. It is built on a firm base, layer by layer, and there should be staggered joints between each layer, enabling the logs to lock together.

This type of wall is not suitable for retaining any great weight of soil and it is not recommended to build it higher than 1.2m (4ft). In order to add strength, alpine plants can be planted between the logs, and these are usually spaced 46–60cm (18–24in) apart. Once these become established, they will help to bind the wall together.

A horizontal, natural log edging wall.

A log block wall.

A post and board raised bed used for growing fruit bushes.

Post and Board Raised Beds

This is probably the simplest and most commonly used method of raised bed construction.

You should use pressure-treated posts 7.5cm (3in) square, and 15×2.5cm (6×1in) pressure-treated sawn timber boards. Although wider or narrower boards can be used if necessary, the thickness of the board should not be any less than 5cm (2in).

There are traditionally two methods used when constructing a post and board raised bed. Both require the posts to be concreted in for maximum strength but differ in the cutting and fixing of the boards.

In many instances, the boards are simply nailed or screwed to the front of the posts, although in situations where there is extreme soil pressure, such as large root systems or where the soil surface is walked on frequently – for example a 'no-dig' vegetable plot – there may be a need for a stronger fixing method to be used. This can be done by fixing the boards behind the posts and cutting the edges of the board to mitres so that they fit flush to the posts. It is essential when cutting the boards to size that you make sure they are long enough for the mitred edges to finish in the middle of the post. Once fixed into position, they should be nailed so that they cannot be pushed out by soil pressure. As with all raised beds,

you should always start at the bottom and work up when fixing the boards into position, checking each layer with a spirit level.

Use of Wooden Cladding

As mentioned previously, log rolls can be used to clad a raised bed wall. However, this is not the only type of material that can be used – other suitable materials include willow hurdles and bamboo screening. How these materials are fixed to the wall depends on the type of material the wall is built from. For instance, with masonry walls, you need to drill into the wall, put in suitable rawlplugs, and then attach with screws. In some circumstances, there may not be sufficient width of material to screw through to attach it, for example bamboo screening. In this type of situation, you will need to tie the material in with wire that should be attached to the screws. If the wall to which the cladding is to be attached is made from wood, either nails or staples can be used depending on the material to be attached.

Cladding can be fixed to either straight or curved walls, although in the case of willow hurdle fencing, it will be necessary to soak it in water for forty hours or more until the hurdles are pliable and can be bent easily into position.

Sleepers laid horizontally to create a raised bed.

Railway Sleeper Beds

As with log walls, railway sleepers can be laid either vertically or horizontally to act as a retaining wall for a raised bed. The horizontal method is probably the most widely used, and consists of laying sleepers in rows in a brickwork fashion, so that the vertical joins are staggered. If this type of wall is to be built to a height greater than two sleepers, it will be necessary to drill through them and drive metal stakes at even intervals through the holes into the ground so that all the sleepers are held in place. Alternatively, obtain some lengths of copper piping or metal bars, bend them to form hoops, place them over the sleepers and drive them into the ground. This technique is a lot easier than the metal spike method and will hold the sleepers in place. Its main disadvantage is that the hoops are visible, unlike the metal spikes which are hidden from view.

Horizontal sleeper beds are ideal in situations where a raised shrub or floral border is required.

Sleepers used vertically to retain a small lawn area.

However, where soil retention is the main priority, a vertical sleeper raised bed might be a better option. This type of bed is constructed by digging a trench deep enough to bury approximately one quarter of the sleeper. You should add on 30cm (12in) for drainage. Fill in the first 30cm (12in) with a drainage layer of broken bricks, gravel or stone. Then, using a line as a guide for a straight wall, or a hosepipe for a curved one, start to lay the sleepers and concrete them in. It may also be necessary to put temporary wooden braces either side of the sleepers to hold them in position, especially where higher walls of 1.2m (4ft) or more are built.

WILLOW BUNDLE PLANTERS FOR POND AREAS

In an existing large pond area there may be a necessity to create a marginal or wetland planting area, and this can be achieved in a shallow side of the pond or lake using willow bundles, which basically consists of some willow brash tied in bundles of approximately 30cm (12in) in length and 60cm (24in) in width. If this method is going to be used in a naturally formed pond, it may be possible to drive in pegs or posts into the pond bed, spacing them at 46cm (18in) intervals. The willow bundles can then be wedged between the posts and tied in position. If the pond has a liner, you will not be able to do this, and instead each bundle will need to be weighed down using stones and built up by placing the bundles on top of each other until you reach the desired height.

Once the wall has been built, the planting area can then be back filled using a 5:2 mixture of loam and coarse washed gravel.

COLD FRAMES

Cold frames are used predominately for propagating, growing on, or protecting plants. A cold frame should south facing in order to attract maximum light and warmth, and the site should be free-standing. The cold frame is basically a rectangular box with the back higher than the front and an open top covered with glass or polythene to maximize light and warmth. Alternatively, a mesh cover can be used when cooler temperatures are required, and protection is needed from birds.

A simple cold frame can be constructed from old timber. One of the easiest ways to build this type of structure is to use sleepers at the front and back of the cold frame, which are then connected together with planks of wood for the side panels that are nailed to the sleepers. The length of these sleepers and the

Willow bundles used to create a wetland planting area.

spacing between the front and back rows depends on the size of the covering you are going to use. The height of the cold frame itself is a matter of personal preference, however, the slope from back to front should be 2.5cm (1in) per 30cm (12in). The majority of glass cold frame coverings are old sash window frames, which can usually be obtained from reclamation yards or demolition sites. However, if using a second-hand frame, always ensure that it is in reasonable condition and does not have any signs of woodworm or rot.

Before the frame is used, it should be sanded down and any holes or cracks filled using exterior wood filler. It should be allowed to dry, and then at least two coats of paint applied, taking care not to get any on the glass surface – it is always a good idea to put masking tape around the edges of the glass before applying any paint. If a mesh is to be used, the frame can be constructed from four pieces of 3.8cm (1½in) square timber, with the length and width dependent upon the size of the frame to be covered. The frame is usually screwed together, and then a narrow gauge galvanized mesh should be cut to size, and attached to the outer side of the frame using staples. This type of frame can also have polythene film attached, although if this is used it will be needed to be replaced on a yearly basis. Plastics are also renowned

for losing heat quickly. Therefore a layer of polythene should be attached to either side of the frame so that there is an air space in between, which will improve heat retention.

This type of frame is very lightweight, and therefore can be blown off in strong winds, which means that some type of securing mechanism needs to be fitted. One method that is often used is to attach hinges to the rear of the frame and a hook at the front.

COMPOST BINS

Compost bins are now a common sight in many gardens, enabling the gardener to recycle garden or kitchen waste. Recycling is very much encouraged in modern society and a range of compost bins are now available to buy. In many areas, councils offer plastic compost bins to residents at reduced prices.

However, if you wish to produce large amounts of compost, building your own wooden bin should be considered. Wooden compost bins have two distinctive advantages over the plastic types. They allow more air movement, which assists in breaking down the organic material, and the open construction allows the compost to be turned easily.

As well as the large box-type bins, you can also

A cold frame base situated next to a greenhouse.

A double box compost bin.

construct 'hidden' compost bins, which usually take the form of beehives or windmills. These are ideal for small gardens, and, unlike other compost bins, they can also act as a feature within the garden.

Situating the Bin

A compost bin should be situated out of direct sunlight and preferably somewhere that is reasonably sheltered. It is usually best to have the compost on the bare ground rather than on a concrete base as this allows worms and micro-organisms from the soil to enter the compost. However, where vast quantities of compost are produced such as on large estates and public gardens, concrete bases are often used because they need to be regularly turned using a tractor and bucket.

CONSTRUCTING COMPOST BINS

Box-Type

Single or multiple bins that have two or more bays can be built. The advantage of the multi-bay system is that it allows you to turn the compost from one bay to another, which helps to break it down. It is also possible, using this system, to leave one bin to mature whilst you are filling a new bay with fresh organic material.

The size and shape of the bin depends upon personal requirements, the size of your garden and where it is to be positioned. Generally, the bins are either square or rectangular, and the bin should be at least 90cm (3ft) in each direction in order to get the best results.

A box-type compost bin, be it a single or multi-unit, basically consists of three solid sides and a front section with removable slats for easy access.

It may also have a solid roof. This is not a necessity but it will prevent the compost getting too wet although it does need to be moist in order for it to mature effectively. It will also help prevent rodents digging into the compost. A polypropylene oven fabric is ideal for this purpose, because it will allow some moisture through, but will also give some protection from excessive rainfall and burrowing rodents.

The materials required for a single compost bin are four posts 10cm (4in) square, four battens 2.5cm (1in) square and enough 15×2.5cm (6×1in) boards for all four sides. The length of the timber required and the number of boards is dependent on the size of the compost bin. If you require more than one bay, you will need to allow for an additional three posts, four battens, and enough boards for two sides and the front for each bay.

Once the materials have been sourced, the next step is to mark the shape and base size of the compost bin on the ground, ensuring that it is square. The posts can then be fixed in position. They can either be concreted in, or post spikes can be used, but whatever the method, it is essential that the posts are straight and in line with each other. The boards for the back and sides can then be nailed into position ensuring that they are level and flush with the far ends of the posts. However, in the case of multi-bay compost bins, the back boards should join in the middle of the posts, unless boards are used that are long enough to cover all the bays without joining. Some experts recommend that gaps should be left between the boards to aid circulation, but this can allow vermin to gain entry and the material to dry out. I have found that the best way is not to leave any gaps between the boards, as the bin will get plenty of air through the top and front and if the compost is regularly turned, this will allow air into it.

Once all the boards have been fixed into position, the square battens can be attached to the inner sides of the front posts. The width of these should be slightly greater than the thickness of the boards in order to allow easy removal for access to the compost. Finally, slide two boards between the battens down to the bottom of the compost bin. You can then start filling the bin with organic matter. Once it is level with the top of the front boards, place another two in position between the battens and continue this process until the compost bin is full.

Pallet

This type of bin is constructed using wooden pallets and consists of using one pallet as a base, and then nailing four pallets together to the base to make a four-sided bin. If you prefer, the bin can be placed directly onto the ground, however, using a base adds stability and can also aid air circulation.

Post and Wire

This is a very simple structure that can be constructed using pressure-treated wood around fence posts and chicken wire. This type of bin is mainly used for leaf composting, but it can also be used to compost other materials if required.

It is built by driving four or more stakes into the

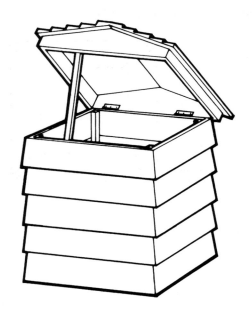

A beehive compost bin.

ground to form a rectangular, square, or round framework. The number of stakes used depends on the size of bin you require. The chicken wire is attached to the posts using staples, except for one edge, which is not attached, as this is to be used as a gate for barrowing in any material to be composted and will be fastened to the post with wire or string when not in use.

Decorative or Hidden

As mentioned earlier in this chapter, there are compost bins that can serve as a decorative feature as well as serving a practical purpose. One of the most effective types, which is relatively simple to construct, is the beehive compost bin. This type of bin is made up of four, five or even six box-section layers that can be lifted off to gain access to the compost. These layers make up the base, on top of which is an apex slatted wooden roof, which also can easily be removed.

In order to construct this type of bin you will need to start by building the base layers. Each layer consists of four 15×2.5cm (6×1in) boards measuring 76cm (30in) on its long side (bottom), and 70cm

Making a beehive compost bin.

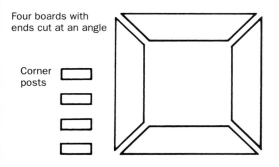

Four boards with
ends cut at an angle

Corner
posts

Timber required for base layers.

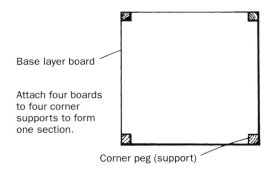

Base layer board

Attach four boards
to four corner
supports to form
one section.

Corner peg (support)

Constructing the base layers.

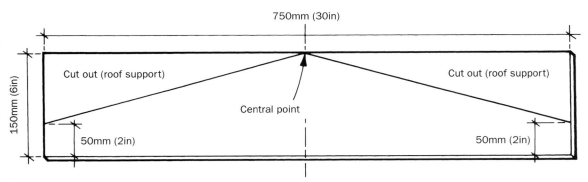

750mm (30in)

150mm (6in)

Cut out (roof support)

Cut out (roof support)

Central point

50mm (2in)

50mm (2in)

Making the gable ends.

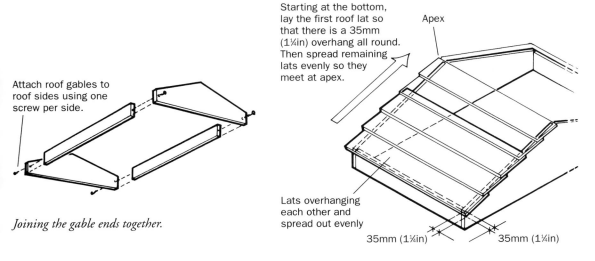

Attach roof gables to
roof sides using one
screw per side.

Joining the gable ends together.

Starting at the bottom,
lay the first roof lat so
that there is a 35mm
(1¼in) overhang all round.
Then spread remaining
lats evenly so they
meet at apex.

Apex

Lats overhanging
each other and
spread out evenly

35mm (1¼in)

35mm (1¼in)

Attaching the laths.

(28in) on its short side with the ends cut at an angle. You will also need four 5cm (2in) square pieces of wood, cut into 15cm (6in) lengths to act as the corner supports.

When all the pieces of wood have been cut to size, attach corner supports at each end on one of the boards with two screws, and then repeat this process on a second board. Line up the remaining two boards and fix with two screws in order to form the first layer. This process should be repeated for the remainder of the layers, and once they have been made up, they should be stacked on top of each other and checked to see if they fit together.

Once the body has put together, it is time to concentrate on constructing the roof section. The two gable ends need to be made from two 15×2.5cm (6×1in) boards, which are 76cm (30in) in length. In order to do this, measure 5cm (2in) high at the end of each board, locate the central point at the top of the board and then draw a line from the points marked at the end of each board up to the central point. This can then be cut and the off-cuts saved. Cut 2.5cm (1in) off the pointed end of the off-cuts to act as the roof supports. Attach one to either end of the inside of both roof gables, 12mm (½in) up from the bottom edge. Next, get two pieces of timber 5cm (2in) square, which should each be 15cm (6in) long. These will act as the handles to enable you to lift off the lid, and should be fixed on the outer side of both of the roof gables in the centre. The two gable ends can now be joined together using two 5×2.5cm (2×1in) pieces of wood. Place the roof section flat on a level surface and attach 10cm (4in) wide feather-board roof laths, which should each be 85cm (34in) long – you will require ten of these. When attaching the roof laths, start at the bottom allowing a 3.8cm (1½in) over-hang, and nail in position. Space the remaining laths evenly so that they meet at the top of the apex, and nail in position.

The roof section is now complete and can be lifted onto the base to finish the project.

CHAPTER 8

Maintenance and Repair

Whilst the previous chapters have looked at the construction processes concerning wooden structures, this chapter will examine the need for correct maintenance, maintenance procedures, and repair techniques.

PESTS AND DISEASES ASSOCIATED WITH TIMBER CONSTRUCTION

The majority of pests and diseases, which includes wet rot, dry rot and many of the wood-boring insects, require moisture to thrive and will only occur in damp timber.

Therefore the simple solution is to eliminate the damp, which will help solve many of the problems.

However, in outdoor wooden structure construction, the exterior, be it a fence, shed or gazebo, is open to the elements. In addition to this, the majority of the structures have some contact with the soil, either through the posts buried in the ground, or because the structure is laid directly on the surface. Also, some of the structures are designed so that plants can climb up them and the plants themselves harbour water. This means that outdoor structures are prone to damp conditions and are, therefore, at a greater risk of being infected by pests and diseases.

Pests

The most common types of pests are wood-boring insects, which are the larvae of certain beetles that lay their eggs on the wood surface. Once the larvae hatch, they bore into the wood and then tunnel through it for up to five years before they pupate and then emerge a few weeks later as adult beetles.

Holes in the surface of the wood do not always mean that you have an active infestation, however if small piles of sawdust are evident, the probability is that it is still active, and an insecticide should be applied to prevent further spreading of this pest.

Diseases

Rot
Timber that remains damp for long periods of time can be attacked by fungi, which will cause decay in the wood, and will eventually make it structurally unsound – this is referred to as rot. The rots are divided into two main groups.

Dry Rot
This is the more serious of the two rots, and is caused by the fungus *Serpula lacrymans*. It does not, as the name may suggest, affect dry wood, as it needs at least 20 percent moisture content within the wood to germinate. This type of fungus can be spread through spores and once it starts to grow, it will go on spreading, not just through wood but over and even sometimes through brick and stone walls and concrete. The other main problem is that once an area is infested, dry wood can also become infected because the threads that spread over the area carry their own water supply. Dry rot is identifiable by its spreading mass of mycelium – tiny white or grey threads that resemble cotton wool or foam. Eventually, large toadstool-type caps form that will

A horizontal log retaining wall showing clear signs of rot.

release more spores. The damaged wood itself looks brown and dry and there may be a lot of red dust that is the spores.

If this type of rot is found, either the affected timbers need to be removed completely, or, if in the middle of a joist, cut out and 46cm (18in) of the unaffected timber on either side should also be removed and replaced. Also, any fungus that has got onto surrounding brickwork, stonework or concrete should be burnt off. In order to prevent a recurrence, the source of the damp should be located, and measures put in place to control it, for example putting a plastic membrane under the joists to prevent the damp rising.

Wet Rot

Whereas dry rot can be caused by only one type of fungus, wet rot is a collective term for thirteen different types of fungi that decay the wood. In order for them to germinate and survive, the wood needs a moisture content above 20 percent. It is less serious than damp rot, in that it will not spread beyond the damp wood, as it does not carry its own water supply. The threads of wet rot are usually brown, and the affected timber may be stained black,

although it is not always easy to distinguish between wet and dry rot. If you are unsure what type of rot you have, check the surrounding area and if you find threads on brickwork, stonework, concrete or other surrounding wood, the probability is that it is dry rot.

As wet rot is not as serious a dry rot and will not spread off the wet timber, the treatment is to scrape out small areas right back into the new wood, or to cut out larger areas, and in both cases the area should be treated with wood preservative.

Preventing Infestation from Pests and Diseases

It is essential in the initial planning stages that ways to help reduce the risk of the timber being over-exposed to damp conditions, and dampness entering the timber, are implemented and this can include the following:

- Use pressure-treated timber, especially in situations where you know there is a high risk of dampness.
- In damp areas ensure that there is adequate drainage. This can include putting layers of gravel underneath posts or bases to prevent water-logging.
- In some situations it may be necessary to give added protection by laying a plastic membrane between the soil or gravel and the wooden structure
- Ensure that where solid roofs form part of the structure, that these are sufficiently clad to give protection, and that they have sufficient fall to allow water run off. There should also be enough overhang on the roof to give some protection to the sides of the structure.
- Even with pressure-treated timber, it is good practice to apply preservative to any areas that are going to be in direct contact with the soil, or which will become inaccessible for maintenance purposes. Posts can be soaked overnight in wood preservative to give added protection, and another coat of preservative should be applied to the structure itself, which will both enhance its appearance and give added protection, especially to areas that have been drilled, nailed, screwed or cut.

APPLICATION OF PRESERVATIVES AND PAINTS

As previously stated, pressure-treated timber should be used for the majority of wooden structure construction, although it will still be necessary to provide additional protection in the form of paint, varnish or a wood preservative applied immediately after the structure has been installed and at regular maintenance intervals after that. Wood stains and preservatives should be applied every two years, and painted areas should be re-coated approximately every five years.

Preservatives

Water-based preservatives are the most commonly used because they are relatively cheap, widely available and will not harm the surrounding vegetation. They are also harmless to humans and pets and if any is spilt it can be washed off. The majority of preservatives also contain stains, which will protect your wood and enhance its appearance.

Water-based preservatives can be applied either with a brush or through a sprayer, but brushing is the usual application method. The advantages of using a brush are that you can get an even coverage, there are less runs and wastage, and smaller, more intricate areas can be covered easily. This is especially important on sheds or other structures where precision work is required, for example around windows and between beams. Brushing also ensures that the preservative gets between the grains, which is especially important when treating new wood. Spraying can also have its uses when applying preservatives to timber and is predominantly used when treating previously treated runs of panel-type fencing, because preservatives can be applied quickly, which is especially important for long stretches.

Whichever method of application is chosen, always rub down the area using a wire brush to remove any loose material prior to treatment. Wash all surfaces with soap and warm water using a stiff brush. The areas to be treated should then be left to dry before applying the preservative.

If you are treating new wood, two coats are usually a minimum requirement, whereas if treating a previously treated surface then one coat may be sufficient. Ultimately, the number of coats is dependent on how absorbent the wood is, and the final decision on this can only be made after each coat has dried.

If applying preservative to previously treated wood then any repair work should be undertaken

A shed that has been partially re-stained as part of its maintenance programme. This picture shows the difference between stained and unstained wood.

first. If some wood has been replaced on an old structure, this may need additional coats in order to match it in with the existing wood.

Paints

The majority of wooden structures tend to be stained rather than painted, although there are situations where a painted finish is preferred such as gates, some types of fences and also wooden buildings that you want to merge in with the house or other painted structures.

Good preparation is essential, because if this is not done correctly, the paint will not adhere to the surface, and blistering and cracking may occur. It does not matter how much paint you apply – any defects below the surface will still be visible, which will in turn spoil the overall visual effect.

If the surface has had previous coats of paint, and it is reasonably sound then wash the entire surface first with soapy water. Once this has been done, roughen the surface with sandpaper to form a

A planter that has not been maintained for at least two years and is in desperate need for a combined stain and preservative to be applied.

receptive surface for the new paint. If there are any damaged areas, these should be sanded and any holes or cracks filled with wood-filler. For damaged paint-work, where sanding will not create a smooth surface, it will be necessary to strip the paint off, which is best done using a scraper and blowlamp. When using a blowlamp, try to avoid concentrating the flame on one spot for too long or it will damage the wood. If the wood does become burnt it will be necessary to sand down the area before painting.

Bare timber should be brushed with a wire brush to remove any loose particles, washed down with soap and water, allowed to dry and then a primer should be applied. You must ensure that the primer is brushed well into the grain and any crevices or indentations, as this will help to give a strong adhesion when fillers are applied. Once the primer is dry it should be sanded down and filled with wood-filler. After the filling has been completed, allow it to dry, and then lightly sand and apply a coat of undercoat. Allow this to dry before applying a top coat.

INSPECTION

Wooden buildings such as sheds, summerhouses or playhouses need to be regularly inspected and maintained.

Annual Inspection

A major inspection is recommended at least once a year, the best time being at the end of the summer. The reason for this is that the structure will have had its main usage during the summer months, and doing an inspection towards the end gives enough time for any maintenance and repair work to be carried out before winter commences. With the onslaught of bad weather, any minor problems such as ripped roofing felt, loose boards or blocked guttering could be made worse if they are not rectified.

Outside
You should be sure to:

• Inspect the condition of the felt and tiles. Check to see if any of the roofing material is damaged and needs either replacing or repair.

The effects of lack of maintenance can be seen clearly on this wooden building.

A newly re-felted shed roof with wooden battens being used to hold the felt in place.

- Look at the fascia boards, ensure that they are not loose and check for any signs of rot. When looking at the guttering, check that it is not loose and connected correctly, and that there are no leaks or blockages. The easiest way to check if the guttering system is working correctly is to pour water into it and check along it to ensure there are no leaks.
- Inspect the walls of the building. This will include checking to see if there is any rot or loose boards. Particular attention should be given to the bottom of the walls, especially where wall panes or posts are touching, or are below the soil surface. It may be necessary to remove some of the soil away from the base of the walls or posts in order to give them a more thorough inspection.

- Check the windows and doors for any rot, loose or broken glass and missing window beading. Make sure that the windows and doors open and close without sticking, that the hinges, window and door fixings work correctly and there are no missing screws or broken parts.

Inside
- Look for signs of woodworm or rot in any of the inside timbers including walls, roof timbers, doors and windows. It is also a good idea to go inside when it is raining and look for signs of dampness where rain is entering the building. Mark these areas with chalk, so that they can be located and repaired.
- The floor area should be carefully checked for

signs of woodworm or rot. Whilst doing this, look out for any loose or broken floorboards and stamp on the floor to check the supporting joists. If the floor appears to be very spongy or bouncy, it may be necessary to lift the floorboards and check the joists for signs of rot. If rot or damage to the joists is found, do not replace the floorboards immediately but schedule this as one of the first repair jobs to be undertaken.

- If the building has any services such as electricity or water, make sure that they are working correctly and that there is no damage to cables, pipes or fittings. If damage is found, the service concerned should be isolated immediately and repairs undertaken.

Spring Inspection

The inspection in the spring months consists of basically looking at the building to see what damage, if any, has occurred during the winter and what repair work is required to prepare the building for summer use.

The entire outside of the shed should be checked for damage, and the inside for any signs of dampness and leaks.

MAINTENANCE

The work identified by the inspections is mainly repair work, and this is usually undertaken within the following two weeks in order to prevent any damage that has been identified from becoming worse. In the case of wooden buildings, the maintenance is normally scheduled for the early spring period ready for summer use, and can be undertaken in conjunction with the spring inspections.

Annual Maintenance

Maintenance requirements can vary according to the building. However, listed below is a general maintenance schedule that can be adapted depending on what type of wooden building you have:

- Clean the roof area, although how this is undertaken depends on the type of roof and material used to cover it. However, as a general guideline, you need to remove any debris, such as twigs and leaves. In the case of felt or tiled roofs, these should be removed with a stiff brush. In cases where there is a build-up of algae and moss there may be a need to use an algae or moss killer.
- Remove leaves and debris from gutters and down-pipes.
- Wash down all the outside walls of the shed, including the door, with warm soapy water and a scrubbing brush.
- Thoroughly clean all the interior of the building, which includes the roof area, walls, floor, and the inside of the door. Soap and water should not be used as this may cause a damp problem in an enclosed area, use a dry soft brush instead.
- Oil all the hinges on the doors and widows, and lubricate any other moving parts such as door locks.

Regular Maintenance

As well as the annual maintenance, there are two jobs that need to be carried out on a regular basis. One of these is the cleaning of glass, which is especially important for structures such as summerhouses where the glass plays a major role in the use and enjoyment of the building.

The other task that should be undertaken on a regular basis is the removal of bird mess, which can spoil the overall look of the structure and can be a big problem, particularly where structures are situated near or underneath trees.

Services

Any services that are supplied to the building such as gas, electricity, and water, should be maintained and repaired only by a professional. Water should be shut down and drained off in situations where there is no heating and it is not going to be used over the winter months.

Decking

For health and safety reasons raised decks, balustrades, steps and staircases should be inspected at least once a month. Ground-level decks probably only need inspecting once a year and this usually undertaken in the spring months. When inspecting deck areas, particular attention should be paid to the following where applicable:

- Decking boards should be checked to ensure that they are not loose, broken or rotting, and replaced as necessary.
- Supporting posts should be thoroughly inspected, especially at the bottom, as this is the most susceptible to rot. If the posts are found to be rotting then they should be replaced immediately. In order to do this, braces should be fitted to either side of the affected post to take the weight of the deck, and then the post can be removed and replaced.
- Balustrades, which are designed to take the weight of a fully-grown adult, are there to stop people falling off the decking and to act as a means of support. They should be checked for any sign of rot or damage, and should be replaced as necessary. Any bolts that are holding the balustrades in position should also be checked and tightened.
- Steps and staircases are potentially lethal if they are not maintained correctly and like supporting posts and balustrades, need to be thoroughly inspected on a regular basis. When inspecting steps or staircases, you need to check any supporting posts, and also the stair treads and handrails to see if they are rotten or loose. If any problems are found, the stairs need to be cordoned off and the problem rectified immediately.

Decks should be treated with two coats of a decking stain and preservative immediately after installation. It is important to choose a high-quality decking stain and preservative that penetrates the wood and contains a fungicide, as this will prevent the growth of algae and moulds, which can make the surface slippery.

After the initial treatment, the deck area will need treating annually and this is best undertaken in early autumn, so that the area is ready for the winter weather. If the decking is not regularly treated, it will soon become faded and grey, and the wet winter weather can cause a lot of damage by swelling and cracking the wood. Therefore, it is recommended that the decking and surrounding timber, including steps and balustrades, are treated by applying a suitable cleansing agent evenly over the surface, working it into the wood with a stiff broom and then it washing it off with a pressure washer or hosepipe. In cases where the wood is very dirty or badly stained, it may be necessary to repeat the treatment. Allow the wood to dry completely, and then clean the surface using a damp cloth and methylated spirits or thinners, which will remove any grease or resinous residues.

After approximately forty-eight hours, apply the decking stain and preservative. Brush in a full, flowing movement in the direction of the grain. Only

This decked area has not been regularly maintained with decking preserver and looks faded and grey, thus spoiling the visual effect.

one board should be treated at a time to avoid overlap marks, and you must ensure that the ends of boards have been treated, as these can be particularly susceptible to water damage.

When all of the decking has been treated, it should then be allowed to dry for at least twenty-four hours or according to the manufacturer's instructions before it is used.

A deck is an area for relaxing and entertaining, and therefore it is somewhere that gets a great deal of use. Some of the things that can damage it include:

- High heels, especially stilettos, or any other sharp objects as these can indent the surface of the wood and damage it.
- Fire – barbecues and candles (especially night-lights) should not be placed directly onto the deck, otherwise they may burn the wood.
- Placing plants in pots around the area. It is essential that these are placed on waterproof trays and slightly raised off the surface, which will prevent staining and allow the wood to breathe.

In order to ensure that the deck area always looks its best, it should be cleaned using a pressure washer at least once a month to remove bird mess and grime.

Fencing

Regular application of wood preservatives is essential to prolong the life of your fence and this is usually undertaken every two years. However, maintenance does not stop here – regular inspections are required as they are for other wooden structures, and the best time to do this is towards the end of summer, so it is ready for the winter weather. Inspections vary for different types of fencing, but as a general rule, the following should be inspected closely.

Fence Posts

If a fence post rots it will eventually collapse and bring down a section of the fence. Therefore, you should inspect the fence posts thoroughly, especially around the base as this is where it is most likely to rot. Particular attention should be paid to the top of the posts as this is an area that can also rot. Where post caps are fitted, these should be checked and replaced as necessary.

A fence post showing signs of rot, being held in place by a round wooden stake.

If a fence post is showing signs of rot, a temporary repair can be made by attaching a wooden brace on either side of the post. However, the only real alternative is to replace the rotten post. To do this, you should carefully remove the fence from the post. Once this has been done, the post can be replaced using the following methods:

- Fence posts that have been driven into the ground using a sledgehammer or similar tool should be dug out, or it can be pulled out if there is enough solid post to allow you to do so. In order to pull out a post, you can use a broom handle and a length of rope. Loop the rope around the post at a height of at least 90cm (3ft) and then tie both ends to the broom handle, leaving approx 20cm (8in) slack. The broom handle should be turned in a clockwise direction until the rope has a vice-like grip against the post, Then, holding the broom handle, lift the post out of the ground.

Removing a fence post using the rope and broom handle method.

- If the post is pulled out of the ground, it may be possible to replace it by hammering a slightly wider post into the same hole. Alternatively, if the post has been dug out, it will be necessary to concrete the new post in. In some cases, such as post and wire fencing, it may be possible to move it slightly away from the old post and then drive it into the ground.
- If a fence post is held in position using a fence spike and the post needs replacing, this is a relatively simple task. The old post should be removed from the post socket. In order to do this, you should slacken off the bolts, and lift the post out of the old socket. The new post can then be slotted into the socket and the bolts tightened.
- If a post has been concreted into the ground, it can be removed by digging it out. However, this method is fairly labour-intensive and sometimes it is not possible to remove it without disturbing or destroying parts of the garden surrounding it. An alternative method is to cut off the fence post level with the base and use a bolt to attach a metal post socket to the old base. Once this has been done, the post can be fixed into position.

Gravel Boards/ Kick Boards

These are positioned at the bottom of the fence panel in order to protect it. Because of where they are situated, there is contact with the soil that can cause them to rot and it may become necessary to replace them before the end of the life expectancy of the fence panels.

Fence Panels

If a fence panel is damaged or is showing signs of rot, the easiest option is usually to replace rather than repair it. Fence panels are available in standard sizes,

An example of a fence panel that needs replacing.

so removing and replacing one is not a difficult operation, and the method used is the same as when erecting a new panel fence.

Fence Boards

Damaged or broken boards will need replacing whatever the type of fence. In the case of fences such as closeboard fencing, where the boards overlap each other, in order to remove a damaged board it will be necessary to loosen the overlapping board. In some situations where there are no gravel boards and a number of vertical fence boards have rotted at the base, if the rot is not too far up the board it may be possible to saw them off along the base.

Another problem associated with board-type fencing, is that undamaged boards can become loose because the nails have rotted. In these circumstances the boards should be refitted using galvanized nails.

Arris Rails

Arris rails that act as the supporting timbers for closeboard fences are susceptible to damage, and may become loose or even crack or break.

The boards on this fence have very visible rot, which is so bad that all the boards need replacing.

If an arris rail is loose, it can be tightened by hammering a wedge of wood coated in wood glue into where the end of the rail joins into the post. If the rails are cracked or broken, two methods can be used. The first is to repair the broken arris rail and the other is to replace it. An arris rail can be repaired if it is cracked; however, if it is more badly damaged or has signs of rot it should be replaced.

In order to repair a cracked rail in the middle you can use a straight arris rail bracket, which is simply a metal bracket approximately 30cm (12in) in length, shaped to fit the rail and attached using screws or nails through the ready-made holes. For cracks that are near to the post, a flanged arris rail bracket is available that can be attached to the post using the flanges, and the straight part connected to the rail.

If it is not possible to repair the rail then it will need to be replaced. In order to do this, knock the boards away from the damaged rail, so that the nails are not attached to it. The rail can then be released, which should be easy to do if the rail is broken. However, if the rail is not completely broken, it will be necessary to cut all the way through it so it can be released.

In order to fit the new rail, cut it longer the length required and shape one end so that it fits into the fence slot. Cut it at the other end so that it will fit flush against the post and fix this end to the post with a flanged bracket.

Pergolas, Gazebos and Similar Structures

These types of wooden structures, like all others, need to be inspected and maintenance work undertaken at least once a year. The best time to do this is in early spring as one of the main functions of these structures is to support climbing plants, and the majority of these are be pruned during the spring period. Once the plants have been pruned, it is easier to inspect and carry out any repair work. When carrying out inspections, particular attention should be paid to timber joints, supporting posts, and the condition of climbing supports. Timber preservative should be applied every two years, but only products that will not harm or kill plants should be used. If possible, any climbers should be detached from their supports ready for treatment. If it is not possible to remove the climbers, loosely cover with a dustsheet or other protective material, and apply preservative to the exposed timber.

Planters, Raised Borders and Similar Areas
Paint, stains and preservatives are usually applied to these structures every two years. In the case of smaller planters, it is also an opportunity to replace and re-pot any plant material. The planters can be emptied and left to dry out then thoroughly inspected. Any treatment, both to the inside and outside of the planter, must be carried out before replanting. The best time to do this is between mid-October and the end of February, as this is when plants are dormant and disturbing the root system will not harm them.

As discussed earlier, there are many different types of raised borders and one of their roles is to retain large amounts of soil. Therefore it is essential that they are structurally sound and it is necessary to carry out three inspections each year. One should take place at the end of the summer, in order to ascertain whether any repair works are required before the onslaught of winter. Heavy rainfall, snow and ice can cause the soil to move, thus putting extra pressure on the supporting structure, which may collapse if it is not in good condition. The next inspection is usually in early spring, and this looks at what damage, if any, has been caused over the winter period. The final inspection is carried out in June or July, or during periods of extreme warm weather. This is especially important in areas where the soil is made up of heavy clay, as during warm weather it dries out and cracks, thus the soil moves, putting increased pressure on the supporting structure.

When carrying out these inspections, all the exposed timber should be examined, and if problems are found such as damage, rot or any movement, dig out behind any timbers where rot is suspected in order to carry out a more detailed inspection before any work is undertaken. However, in some cases, especially with older structures, and where there is no sign of any soil movement, it may be better not to disturb the soil but simply to monitor the situation, as the soil may now be held place with plant roots. In these situations, it may not be necessary to repair the structure because any disturbance of the soil may make the problem worse. As well as inspecting raised

Detach climbers from supports in order to apply preservative to exposed timbers.

Dig out behind any timbers where rot is suspected in order to carry out a more detailed inspection.

The woven fencing used to clad a block wall is showing signs of rot and needs replacing.

beds that are in direct contact with the soil, it is also necessary to inspect walls that are cladded with a wooden covering as these can also rot and may need repairing or replacing.

Regular maintenance basically consists of applying preservative, stain or paint approximately every two years to exposed timbers.

Compost Bins and Cold Frames

The best time to inspect either compost bins or cold frames is when they are empty so that the general framework can be looked at and any repair work carried out. It is important to inspect the covers of cold frames every time they are used especially if they are glazed, because if the glass is damaged or

the frame holding it has been weakened, this can pose a risk to the health and safety of people using it. A damaged cover should, therefore, be repaired immediately, or removed and stored in a secure place.

Regular maintenance is fairly straightforward and basically involves the application of wood preservatives, which is best undertaken when the structures are empty.

SUMMARY OF CONSTRUCTION, INSPECTION, REPAIR AND MAINTENANCE PROCEDURES

Whatever the type of wooden structure, the procedures for construction, inspection, repair and maintenance can be summarized as follows:

- It is of the utmost importance that any type of wooden structure is properly constructed, and that the correct size of timber and fittings are used. As a general rule for outside work, pressure-treated timber should be used, and where this is damaged or cut during the construction process, additional preservative should be applied.
- Carry out regular inspections, and repair any damage as soon as possible to prevent it getting worse.
- Do not neglect regular maintenance work, such as applying timber preservatives and paints, or this will spoil the appearance, cause unnecessary repair works and generally shorten the lifespan of the wooden structure.

By observing these guidelines, you will ensure that whatever the structure, it will look good for years to come and also give many years' service.

Further Reading

Hislop, P.J., *External Timber Cladding* (TRADA Technology, 2000)
Provides guidance on the choice of timber species and profiles for cladding configuration.

Littlewood, M., *Landscape Detailing, Volume 1, Enclosures* (3rd Ed.) (Architectural Press, 1993)
Covers not just wooden structures, but also provides invaluable information for all those thinking of constructing enclosures such as fences, gates, barriers, bollards and walls. It includes technical notes on design and construction, and drawn-to-scale detail sheets.

Littlewood, M., *Landscape Detailing, Volume 3, Structures* (3rd Ed.) (Architectural Press, 1997)
Covers pergolas, arbors, arches, gazebos, summerhouses, sheds, shelters, decks, footbridges, furniture and roofs. It also includes technical notes on design and construction, and drawn-to-scale detail sheets.

Useful Contacts

BSI (British Standards Institute)
389 Chiswick High Road
London
W4 4AL
Tel: 0208 996 9000
www.bsi-global.com

Independent quality certification of management systems and products.

BWPDA (British Wood Preserving and Damp-Proofing Association)
1 Gleneagles House
Vernon Gate
Derby
DE1 1UP
Tel: 01332 225101
www.bwpda.co.uk

Nationally recognized authority on timber and damp problems.

British Woodworking Federation
55 Tufton Street
London
SW1P 3QL
Tel: 0870 458 6939
www.bwf.org.uk

The leading representative body of the woodworking industry.

The Landscape Institute
33 Great Portland Street
London
W1W 8QG
Tel: 0207 299 4500
www.l-i.org.uk

The Chartered Institute in the UK for Landscape Architects

TRADA (Timber Research and Development Association)
Stocking Lane
Hughenden Valley
High Wycombe
Bucks
HP14 4ND
Tel: 0124 024 2771
www.trada.co.uk

TRADA maintains the UK's largest research programme directed entirely at building markets and for influencing the specification of timber and other wood-based products.

WMSA (Woodworking Machinery Suppliers Association)
The Counting House
Mill Road
Cromford
Derbyshire
DE4 3RQ
Tel: 01629 826998
www.wmsa.org.uk

WMSA heads the Working with Wood Confederation, a group of trade associations spanning the woodworking industry supply chain.

Index